Radionics
and
Progressive
Energies

by Keith Mason M.Rad.A.

THE C.W. DANIEL COMPANY LTD
1 Church Path, Saffron Walden
Essex, England

First published in Great Britain by
The C.W. Daniel Company Limited
1 Church Path, Saffron Walden, Essex, England.

ISBN 0 85207 160 4

Typesetting by Simpson Typesetting, Bishop's Stortford, Herts.
Printed by Whitstable Litho, Whitstable, Kent.

For Chrissy
My thanks for your continued
support and encouragement

ACKNOWLEDGEMENTS

To Richard Belsham for providing the line diagrams of instruments. The C.W. Daniel Company Ltd, Saffron Walden: *Radionics and the Subtle Anatomy of Man, Dimensions of Radionics, Radionics: Science or Magic?*, all by David V. Tansley D.C. Steiner Press: *Fundamentals of Therapy* by Rudolph Steiner. The C.W. Daniel Company Ltd: *Heal Thyself* by Edward Bach, M.D. The Lucis Press: *Treatise on Cosmic Fire* by Alice Bailey. The Theosophical Publishing House: *Secret Doctrine* by Mdme Blavatsky. The Radionics Association: *Introduction to Subtle Anatomy* by Daphne de Salis. The Lucis Press: *Esoteric Psychology 1 and 2* by Alice Bailey. Dr Aubrey Westlake: *Pattern of Health*. Routledge & Kegan Paul Ltd: *Psionic Medicine* by J.H. Reyner & Dr Lawrence. The Lucis Trust: *Esoteric Healing* by Alice Bailey. *The C.W. Daniel Company Ltd:* Vaccinosis by Compton Burnett M.D. The Steiner Press: *Spiritual Science and Medicine* by Rudolph Steiner. The C.W. Daniel Company Ltd: *Divination of Disease* by H. Tomlinson, M.D. American Journal of Acupuncture, Vol 8: *Electro Acupuncture* by Dr Voll. Stuart & Watkins: *Life Threatened* by Dr Aubrey Westlake. Dragons World Ltd: *The Round Art* by A.T. Mann. Routledge & Kegan Paul: *Diving the Primary Sense* by Herbert Weaver. Thorsons *Healing with Radionics* by L. Dower & E. Baerlein. Journal of the Research Society for Natural Therapeutics: *Homoeopathy Up-to-Date* by Malcolm Rae. White Eagle Publishing Trust: *Planetary Harmonies* by Joan Hodgson. Books from India: *Gem Therapy* by Bhattacharya. L.N. Fowler & Co., Chadwell Heath: *Heal Thyself* by M. MacDonald Bayne.

CONTENTS

6

LIST OF ILLUSTRATIONS

GLOSSARY OF ABBREVIATIONS USED WITH MAGNETO GEOMETRIC APPLICATION PRINCIPLES AND PROTOCOL

M G A	Magneto geometric applications
C N S	Central nervous system
S N S	Sympathetic nervous system
P S M S	Para-sympathetic nervous system
G I.TRACT	Gastro-intestinal tract
N D P F	No detectable Prior Factor
SOLAR P	Solar plexus chakra
ALTA M	Alta Major chakra
WITNESS	Sample of patient's hair, blood spot, urine sample
G T C	Group Treatment Card
E R	Extended Range Instrument
T C C	Therapeutic Command Cards

Introduction

During the last few years, many books have been written on the subject of Radionics, but few have put down in print a procedure for using instruments and the radiesthetic faculty in practising the art of Radionics.

In the chapters that follow, it will be shown how the radiesthetic sense, the use of the instruments and the pendulum are not solely for the Radionic Practitioner, but can be used, as is happening already, by many health care professionals.

For example, the Osteopath and Chiropractor can confirm their diagnosis when searching for the areas of the skeletal system needing adjustment. A dentist with a holistic approach can use the radiesthetic faculty in finding the cause or focus of inflammation in the mouth – in fact, the oral cavity may be of major importance when searching for causative factors in a patient's malady, for the problem may originate in part from an infected tooth or tonsillar area.

We shall discuss the Dr Bach Flower remedies and the Seven Rays, including the selection of the correct flower remedy, which flowers have a healing relation to particular areas of the subtle bodies, and how the remedies will help a patient heal himself or cope with the conflict within.

The Homoeopath too, can be aided in his remedy selections. It is important that a connection or interface be developed between the Radionic Practitioner and the Homoeopath, for both are dealing with the vital forces of the patient and the vital forces of the healing remedies, be they homoeopathic, biochemic or Bach flower remedies.

Related to this connection between the two professions, is their understanding of the Miasms as a causative factor in disease, and how to help the patient eradicate the Miasm or let it flow from the higher bodies into the etheric field of the earth.

I will be dealing in detail with the use of Radionic instruments for analysis and treatment, and will be using a great deal of material prepared by the late Malcolm Rae.

It will be shown how the health care professional can use Radionics in his practice, that a great deal of work is to be done in the field of allergies and the allergic reaction and how allergies have their origin in the Subtle Anatomy of Man.

There are many excellent works on the Subtle Anatomy of Man, particularly those of Dr David Tansley, and the use of this Subtle Anatomy knowledge is of paramount importance if one is to practise Radionics with success.

During visits to Australia and the United States the writer met many health care professionals using Radionics, not as a sole healing therapy but as an adjunct to their existing practices.

This is an area where the qualified Doctor has at his disposal immense healing energy. He can, from his understanding and practical education in physical anatomy, visualise what is required within the patient. He can direct the healing energies to exactly where they are required. I have met many highly qualified Doctors who use Radionics for analysis and treatment with great success.

What is of importance in health care today is the counselling of the patient, whether it be face to face or by correspondence.

Radionics allows the practitioner to establish the path on which the patient treads, and how to cope with the problems he faces. All too often today the patient is left to his own devices after being prescribed the allopathic drugs to sedate or change his moods. Human contact and the knowledge that the practitioner cares is all important.

This book, I trust, will benefit the lay practitioner and those beginning in Radionics, as well as those health care professionals that use Radionics daily.

The material contained and the references in this book have been used for many years in my practice. I offer them to you as a basis for helping your patient obtain optimum health.

The procedures explained are given as a guide and they can be built upon to suit your own needs whatever your therapy may be.

In building up our understanding of Radionics and the

radiesthetic sense, we must be fully aware of what we are doing when preparing an analysis or giving treatment.

Malcolm Rae suggested that when the word Radionics was coined as a word, no one at that time knew whether it was the instrument, the rates, the cards with the partial radii, or the operator, that enabled the analysis to be prepared and the treatment to be given. Many hypotheses have been put forward on this subject. My own interpretation is that the practitioner in the use of the radiesthetic sense is using the supersensible knowledge that is possessed by all, but in many is dormant. This supersensible knowledge reveals to us, when we contact our patient at the higher levels of consciousness, the causative factors of their disease. Dr David Tansley refers to this area as the concept of right brain function and holistic mentation, when the practitioner can contact the patient in this particular realm, but only when left brain logic has been satisfied; with this I agree entirely.

Radionics and the radiesthetic sense is used to tap the divine consciousness, the source of all knowledge, from which information will be given to the enquirer, based on correct questioning and intent.

Radionics, I consider, is a form of spiritual healing that uses mathematical concepts in conjunction with instruments, enabling the practitioner to find the root cause of any symptom or condition. He can treat the cause again with mathematical concepts in conjunction with instruments that will arouse the vital forces in the patient. This information can be administered to the patient by Radionic Therapy alone, or by the use of the homoeopathic or Flower remedies, all of which are vehicles for the divine spark of information gleaned from the supersensible fields, to activate the vital forces within the patient.

Although comprehensive medical dictionaries contain named diseases which run into thousands, these are no more than names attached to clinically recognisable sets of symptoms, and do not generally relate to the causes which are fewer in number. I am convinced that in Radionic therapy, or in Radionics used as an adjunct to a practitioner's own therapy, basic simplicity is what is needed in searching for the causes of the patients anomalies.

I believe there are no more than five fundamental causes of illness which can develop in an initially healthy individual; these are:

(a)   Detrimental substances in the body, superfluities in too great a quantity, toxins and poisons, resultants from autointoxication.

(b)   Deficiencies: the absence of substances needed by the body for growth, and normal maintenance and repair.

(c)   Psychosomatic complaints, or the conflict between the soul energies and the personality, the individual's failure to come to terms with life, uncoordination of the Mental, Astral and Etheric Body.

(d)   Mechanical injury and damage to the body.

(e)   Environmental stress, having to live and work in surroundings which place on the individual stresses greater than those for which he was designed.

It is with these concepts of basic simplicity, the use of the radiesthetic faculty in establishing the causative factors, the knowledge of where the causes can lie and how to treat them with Radionics and other therapies, that the following chapters are written. My theories, opinions and procedures have grown from a combination of reading, thought and radiesthetic investigation and discussion with many health care professionals. This means that in the following chapters I may inadvertently describe something as if it were original, when in fact it has been previously described by another investigator or therapist. If so, I offer my apologies – for me it was original, and the procedures described are based on my own practice methods.

Keith Mason M.Rad.A.
Gate Cottage,
Sandy Balls Estate,
Godshill,
Fordingbridge, Hants.

January, 1984

CHAPTER ONE

Man and his Spiritual Origins

*"The physical organism alone could never call forth a process of
self healing: it is in the etheric organism that the process is
kindled"*

Rudoph Steiner
Fundamentals of Therapy

A primary requisite of all those wishing to use Radionic
Practice as a healing art is the ancient dictum, "know thyself" –
the attainment of self-knowledge and insight, as the truth and
answers that arise in the practitioner's mind when seeking causes
must now come from within, rather than, as hitherto, from the
material world without. Radionic Practitioners must have a
sound basic knowledge of physiology and physical anatomy, to
act as the foundation in questioning through the radiesthetic
sense, and making contact with the supersensible world.

This is not going to be easy, for the educational processes
today are governed by the materialistic outlook on life, and only
when the Subtle Anatomy of man is studied and fully
understood, can the nature of the etheric organism be awakened
in practitioner and patient alike.

Dr Bach in his book *Heal Thyself* says, "Disease is in essence
the result of conflict between Soul and Mind, and will never be
eradicated except by spiritual and mental effort." This again is an
indication as to where the radionic practitioner must make his
investigations, since all diseases, barring mechanical injury, have
their origins in the Subtle Body.

Years before Christ was born, physicians working in ancient

India under the direction of Lord Buddha, advanced the art of healing through knowledge of the spiritual aspect of man to a state when surgery, efficient as it was in that day, was abolished. Other great men such as Hippocrates and Paracelsus, both certain of the divinity of man, and Samuel Hahnemann, the founder of homoeopathy, all had the realisation of the beneficent love of the Creator and of the Divinity which resides within man. Samuel Hahnemann, by studying the mental attitudes of his patients towards life, the environment and their respective diseases, sought to find in herbs of the field and in other realms of nature, remedies that would heal their bodies and uplift their spiritual and mental outlook.

Dr Bach gave to us in the use of the flower remedies the ability to help our patients in the area of the etheric body and to eradicate the causative imbalances and thus in turn heal the physical body. The physical organism is always striving for perfection and with the correct instruction to the vital forces of the etheric field of man the dynamic balance can be restored, and physical symptoms will dissipate.

The most prolific writer on Subtle Anatomy is Dr David Tansley and it is vital that all practitioners should read and fully understand his work, as it is a basis on which to build the understanding of where the practitioner should begin his investigations when using Radionics.

The chapters that follow on in this book that concern the procedures of Subtle Anatomy analysis are written with the assumption that the reader has a basic knowledge of the Etheric and the Spiritual origins of man. However, I will outline some of these basic facts and references to where readers can further their knowledge on the subject.

The origin of man and his dense physical body originates from a complex array of forces and fields of energy that start in the field of the first cosmic ether, that is the flame of the divine supreme being, the Father or Godhead.

It is said that man is a reflection of the creator and that Jesus Christ, the son of God, was made in his image, therefore it is shown in the diagram taken from *The Treatise on Cosmic Fire* by Alice Bailey (see Fig. 1) that the first spark of man's being originates in the Monadic plane, where the Father, Son and Spirit

MAN'S COSMIC ORIGINS

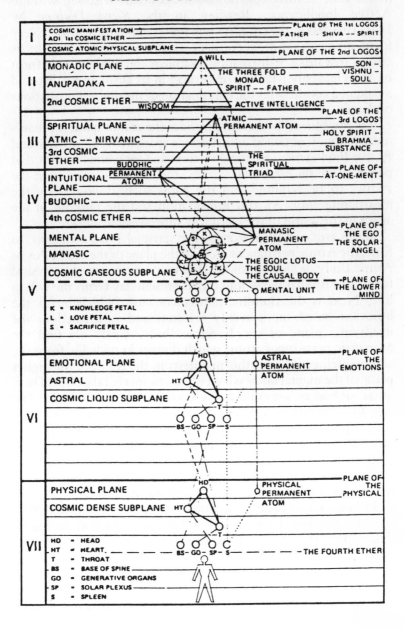

manifest in the three-fold monad and combine Wisdom, Will and Active Intelligence. Reading in the *Secret Doctrine* by H.P. Blavatsky, the enquirer will find statements such as "Every form on earth, and every speck (atom) in space, strive in its efforts towards self-formation to follow the model placed for it by the Heavenly Man". The Monad in its absolute totality and awakened condition is the culmination of the divine incarnations on Earth.

It is the Monad body that provides the divine spark for man's incarnation. Contained in that divine spark of Wisdom, Will and Active Intelligence, are the directives and total blueprint for that person's life on earth: the virtues, the vices and glamours, the virtues to be acquired and the paths to be followed by the incarnating soul. All this information and the purpose of life arises in the world of the spirit, the supersensible world.

In this area of higher worlds, the Spiritual Triad manifests, to form the Atmic permanent atom in the plane of the 3rd Logos or Atmic Body, which builds the Will to incarnate into the physical form; this is what we would call in present day terms the will to live. Next is the Buddhic permanent atom which builds the intuition based on heavenly wisdom and is situated in the intuitional plane or the Buddhic Body. Lastly we find the Manansic permanent atom, which derives knowledge from the active intelligence, and this manifests in the realm of the higher plane of the mental body which is also the level of the Soul. These areas, or bodies, are collectively known as the causal body. The word Bodies is to be used loosely, as these bodies constitute a vast network of energies which are in all forms. Subtle Bodies are in fact not bodies as we would imagine in the physical, or as the dictionary defines the word. They can be looked upon as a reservoir of particular types of forces that are attached to each individual, a collection of atoms vibrating at very high speed.

The causal body and its functions are best viewed as described by Mrs Daphne DeSalis in her brief introduction to Subtle Anatomy: "It is the centre of egoic consciousness, it is neither subjective or objective, it is the accumulation of the good in each incarnation and is a very slow and gradual process. The structure has been built up over a long period, and each stone of the structure has been extracted and dug from the personal lives of the past, and so the path from probation to initiation continues, beautifying and completing the causal body."

Man works in the causal body with the forces of evolution, to build his own character, to cultivate these qualities that he knows are lacking: he strives with the help of soul dictates to bring his personality under control, and to enhance the causal body to become a worthwhile receptacle for the Christ principle. Obviously we as practitioners cannot treat in this area or body, but we can by the radiesthetic sense and use of supersensible knowledge ascertain information that will be of great assistance in directing and counselling the patient on the path of life. It is from this body that certain causative factors emanate, and here predispositions or Miasms can be seated. The Seven Rays and the information conveyed emanates from this area also. This is the area of the patient's free will, not to be interfered with, but to be tapped for its vast quantity of information.

There is a dividing line between the causal body and the plane of the lower mind, a line like the diaphragm in the physical. It divides the higher fields of life energies from the more mundane activities. The division occurs through the Mental Body, and divides this body into higher and lower activity; it separates the intuitional from the logic, it is the rainbow bridge, or link between the left and right brain.

Above the division line in the Mental Body resides the Soul with its nine petals, three of love, three of knowledge and three of sacrifice. All these petals of energy derive their information from the Atmic, Buddhic and Manansic Permanent Atoms, all of this being the totality of the causal body.

Below the diaphragm in the Subtle Bodies is the plane of the lower mind or mental body, the astral or emotional body and the physical etheric body. These three dynamic bodies make up the lower self. This area of combined energies is reacting to the directives of the person's soul, and all energies and forces emanate from the soul petals, to govern that person's life in the physical form as well as the mental and emotional states.

This area of the lower self is also subjected to the environmental forces of the earth, toxins, poisons, miasms and reactive relationships with other human beings.

It is in the low self where the uncoordination, overstimulation, congestion and blockages of energies occur that cause havoc in the chakra centres, and the endocrinology of the body.

Alice Bailey speaks of, "A Man being regarded as a personality in truth when the form aspect and the soul nature are at one".

Coordination between Mental, Astral and Etheric bodies is the prime aim of the soul nature. It is only when the personality is led away from soul dictates that disharmony manifests in the Subtle Bodies and finally results as disease in the physical.

Alice Bailey goes on to say, "when the soul influences the personality and pervades all the lower manifestations, then and only then does the personality measure up to its true significance, which is to constitute the mask of the soul, that which is the outer appearance of inner spiritual forces. These forces are expressions of the soul, and the soul is the central identity or fundamental focus upon the mental plane of the life of God Himself."

Essence, consciousness and appearance are the three aspects of divinity and of Man. The personality, when fully developed, is the appearance of God on earth. Life, quality and form is another way of expressing this same triplicity.

The Mental Body when guided by the dictates of the soul will react to and learn from situations placed upon it by life. Vital reactions to vital forces is what is desired; these should be developed as a state of longing for mental consciousness, intelligent and enquiring thinking processes, intellectual sensitivity and response to thought currents which will bring about a steady but vigorous reaction to the impact of ideas. Clarity of the mental body will only come about when dictates of the soul are set free and uncoordination, congestion and blockages eliminated.

Man very often gets bogged down in his attempts to fulfil the soul dictates and Radionic Therapy has the power to help, along with homoeopathy and Flower Remedies in particular.

When a soul is incarnating and building the necessary subtle bodies for fulfilling the tasks on earth, it builds the bodies of the lower self and certain chakra centres in a particular pattern.

Reference to the diagram on page 17 (Fig. 1) shows that in the plane of the lower mind or lower mental body there are four chakra centres and a mental unit. The energies for these centres emanates from the Soul centre and the Nine Soul Petals.

The Base chakra in the Mental Body plane derives its energies and directives from the Atmic Permanent Atom in the Spiritual plane and the Will aspect of the Three Fold Monad.

The Base Chakra is the seat of the Will, and the Mental Body Base chakra centre gives man the will to live.

The Base Chakra often houses the predispositions or Miasms that have been sent from the Spiritual and Monadic planes. These Miasms are the forces that the soul has to eradicate, and thus predisposes the physical to certain disease patterns that have been acquired by the spirit in previous incarnations. These have to be eliminated before perfection of spirit can be obtained.

The generative organs centre or Sacral Chakra is also part of the plane of the lower mental body and is the energy centre that derives its activities from the knowledge petals of the soul and the Manastic Permanent Atom. This perhaps is where a lot of the genetic codes and information for the building of the body comes from.

Miasms can also be seated in the Sacral chakra or any of the Mental body areas; I have often found them in the Solar Plexus at the mental level.

The Solar Plexus chakra of the Mental Body level is a combination of love, intuition and wisdom. It is through this centre that we experience many of the frustrations and desires of today's world.

The Spleen Chakra on the Mental level is connected esoterically with the Mental unit which is the total blue-print of our life to come. The Mental unit centre contains all that which is a person's total life and is directly connected to the soul centre, and when perfected man of the lower self works through this centre, he can be at total unison with the soul and can cross the antahkarana bridge – the corpus callosum – the total affinity between left and right brain functions and the upper and lower mental levels.

Alice Bailey, in *Esoteric Psychology* speaks of "the fusion of lower energies (astral and mental) and when dominant the personality gets a vision of its destiny, which is the instrument of a higher force." This is the mental unit.

The Monad Body is the source of man's incarnation via the soul to the physical body. The path of return is centred on the higher mental matter or the mental unit, where the inspiration for the return is yet again the Monad.

We enter the lower self through the soul and exit through the mental unit or higher mental matter to return to the Monad.

This is why when working with Radionics it is important to investigate the plane of the lower mind and ascertain the development and functioning of that part of the Mental body.

The Astral body, or emotional plane, is the vehicle of the feeling energy or sensitive force.

It is from the Astral body that all emotions, pleasures and pain are felt, love, hate, serenity, anger and frustration which are so prevalent today. These are all registered and measurable in this body. It is this Astral body that we have to learn to control, for lack of control leads to selfishness, greed, lust and desire for materialism, and leads man away from soul dictates.

Glamour is reflected in this body by the desire to serve, or to do good work; it can reflect as self-pride. True service should be spontaneous with no thought of oneself.

Most individuals today are functioning very potently through this body, and as a result much disease stems from the chaotic reactions between the energies within it.

It is in the Astral body that we have interplay from seven chakra centres. We can see from diagram 1 that the head chakras first manifest in the Astral body receiving their energies from the Base chakra of the mental body. Also the throat chakra and heart chakra have their origins in the Astral, deriving their energies from Mental body Sacral and Solar Plexus centres. The centres of the higher fields of man, that is head chakra, throat and heart, those above diaphragm level, all appear in the Astral body, but still come via the soul.

It is in the Astral body where we first experience the effects of what mental body energy centres inflict on the Astral. As an example we can have Base chakra energies related to deviations in the head centres, so often we treat problems of the head by working on mental base chakra.

The Physical Etheric body directs energy into the physical body to revitalise it, and in so doing integrates the physical into the etheric body of the earth, and the solar system. Dr Tansley states in *Dimensions of Radionics*, which was completed in collaboration with the late Malcolm Rae and Dr Aubrey Westlake: "The etheric body is conditioned and does not condition"; also, "The etheric body is the physical and the problems that arise in it come from the Astral and mental levels."

The physical etheric body has three basic functions, all closely interrelated. It acts as a receiver of energies and assimilates energies from the astral and mental bodies, and is also a transmitter of energies into the physical. If each of these functions is maintained in dynamic balance then the physical body will remain in a state of good health.

Paramount in the etheric body are the energy or chakra centres that are vortices of vitality lying along the spinal column. All of these centres are related to the centres previously described in the astral and mental bodies.

The spleen centre is in a category of its own as it is fundamentally concerned with the vitalisation of the lower-self, drawing in pranic energy from the solar system before distributing the energy to the other centres, and the vitalisation of the etheric body.

The etheric body, being a receiver, an assimilator and transmitter of energies, has between it and the physical the NADIS. These are tiny channels of force which underlie the entire physical etheric nervous system.

These energies vitalise the nerve endings directly and it is said when twenty one or more of these Nadis cross there is an energy or chakra centre.

It is the totality of the Physical Etheric, the Astral and Mental bodies that make up the energies and control the energy centres in the lower self. The soul resides in the plane of the upper mental body and is within the causal body that is constituted by the combination of the Buddhic, Atmic and Monadic Planes. The physical organism is the totality of all these energies, and any healing process that is to benefit the physical body must be kindled in the etheric organism. These energy areas, briefly described, are the vital forces of man and his spiritual origins.

Emanating from these areas in the higher world are many predispositions or Miasms, and it is important for the soul to work these energies out, or let them flow in a way not necessarily

24

to the detriment of the individual or his physical body. These energies cannot just be eliminated.

CHAPTER TWO

The Miasms – Let them Flow

"When the blockages have been removed the flow of forces remains to be restored."

Dr A.T. Westlake:
The Pattern of Health

The term Miasm was first used by Hahnemann, the founder of homoeopathy, and his explanation was that an entity appeared which was non-physical, but had the power to produce ill health by the imbalancing of the protein in the body. Miasms might be described as the etheric counterparts of the original "causal body" (described in Chapter 1) whether microbic or virus, and as such are the main cause of chronic disease.

Practitioners of Radionics and Homoeopathy now know this to be the truth. It is the method of handling these energies from miasms that still causes practitioners many problems.

Many schools of thought, after establishing the presence of a Miasm, will propose a treatment based on a concept of elimination, thus hopefully allowing the body to restore balance to the physical organism; this does not, however, seem to be successful. My personal opinion is that the energies of a miasm should be worked with and allowed to flow through this etheric organism. I do not believe we can eliminate a force such as resides in a miasm.

Such forces that are of an etheric nature can be mobilised and allowed to flow from the higher bodies of man, through to the etheric of the earth, perhaps from where they first came.

Returning to Hahnemann, he found that with his best

intentions, and using homoeopathic similimum, that he was not fully successful with certain types of chronic disease. He observed that these diseases, even after being repeatedly and successfully treated by the then-known homoeopathic remedies, continually reappeared, sometimes in a modified form. This is often what happens when Radionic Practitioners administer their healing energies via their instrumentation: patients' symptoms are ameliorated for a period, but then re-appear. It is fundamental knowledge that the presence of disease implies a departure from a harmonious relationship of the vital energies of the patient. Therefore, the prescribing of homoeopathic remedies, which themselves contain the appropriate energies, or the radionic energies using cards or rates, should restore the balance and so effect a cure.

But sometimes this fails, and we have to ask why.

I am convinced that consideration should be given to why man has to cope with miasms at all. It is often in his casual body that we find their origins, therefore it is a dictate of a person's soul that they should experience the effects during that lifetime that the miasm will give them. By using the homoeopathic remedy and radionic rates in a slightly modified form we can use the forces of these miasms to benefit the person, and allow them to cope with the effects more easily and to eradicate the imbalances much more quickly. The clue to this form of treating miasms was given to me by Dr A. Westlake, where he says "When the blockages have been removed the flow of forces remains to be restored".

What we do is treat the blockage or miasm with the prescribed remedy and direct it through the patient's etheric in a very systematical way. We can modify the effect of the miasm by adding the homoeopathic remedy, the colour, the rate or whatever vital force is appropriate to the force of the miasm, and cleanse the etheric body of the patient, removing the blockages on the way, and allowing a free flow of energy, through the chakra centres, through the endocrine glands and cellular body structures. We can return the miasm to the etheric body of the earth and thus cleanse the patient totally of the taints of the miasmic forces, but we can only do this over a period of time or space as directed or permitted by the patient's own free will, or soul dictates. This is why radionic analysis must include investigation into the causal body dictates.

These aspects of analysis and treatment of miasms will be discussed in more detail in later chapters.

It is pertinent at this time to quote from *Psionic Medicine* by J.H. Reyner, in which he says "The Miasmic theory of chronic disease has never gained adequate recognition in orthodox circles, mainly because it is not understood. The idea, indeed, has become quite incorrectly interpreted by the Homoeopathic Faculty, which defines miasms as specific parasitic infection by micro-organisms. But this is confusing effect with cause, and to equate miasms with microbes is a misinterpretation of Hahnemann's intuitive insight."

He was unable to formulate his ideas precisely in the terms of the limited medical and scientific knowledge of his time, but the development of homoeopathy, simulation, bio-chemistry and dowsing have made possible a new and very practical basis of understanding.

It is by dowsing in the etheric body that inroads can be made into the understanding of the miasm and its effects on the human organism. It can be demonstrated by the radiesthetic faculty that miasms are not only present in the subtle bodies of man but also in the soil itself. Plants grown on that soil contain miasmic traits, as do the animals and humans that feed upon them. Also for consideration is the excreta of animals and the humans themselves that go back to the soil, so that we can see the cycle of forces and energies remains complete and continuous.

An area of miasms that needs a lot of investigation and research is the continued and frightening use of mood-changing drugs used in allopathic medicine so flippantly today. Consider the vast amounts of drugs that are not consumed by the patient, but are flushed down the toilet to be assimilated into the sewerage system, only to be processed by chemical purification for human consumption. What of the mood-changing energies now returning to us in our water supply?

What of the effects on the Astral body of man?

What of the effect when vast numbers of people come together in emotionally charged situations and all of them continually partaking of a minute dosage of a mood-changing influence? I have seen it in the media of today, for example soccer crowd violence, and mob hysteria. Many are the reports in newspapers and on television. This problem, of course, is not restricted to the individual; this is a group problem, of group consciousness, the effects and ramifications of which are yet to be felt as orthodox medicine continues its rampant use of these insidious drugs.

It would appear then that a miasm is some form of non-physical functional dynamic state, as it is clear it is not the same as the actual micro-organism.

It appears to be what is left behind after the organism as such has disappeared, but for practical purposes let us regard it as a wave form or pattern which has the power to produce ill health. It is a deviation from the norm, or deviation from the patient's own soul ray influence which affects optimum function of particular areas of the etheric or physical body.

Most miasms appear to be inherited, in the form of forces passed from one generation to another etherically speaking, or taints from that person's own previous incarnation not eradicated during that previous lifetime.

Miasms, as already shown, can be acquired from the etheric body of the earth during this lifetime, from feeding on plants or animals that contain such forces.

Malcolm Rae was adamant that the forces of fear that occurred in animals prior to slaughter resided in the meat only to be eaten by humans. These forces in particular affect the adrenal gland function of man, as the fight and flight mechanism of the animal aroused potent energies in its bloodstream, that now affect man through his base chakra on an Astral level.

During radiesthetic investigation the writer has found individuals with various miasms in the etheric body that are flowing freely throughout the energy centres into the etheric body of the earth, without having any detrimental effect on the patient's health.

It is only when mental or emotional shock, or injury to the physical body, cause blockages, and thus dam up the forces that are flowing, that congestion of certain energy centres is the result, and malfunction of the endocrine glands a reality.

Could this be an explanation for why a person previously in a good state of health, after suffering a physical injury or emotional shock is within a few months debilitated by some incurable illness, such as cancer, diabetes or even multiple sclerosis?

In very basic terms the energy centres that reside on the spinal column can be likened to the lightning conductor of the church steeple. When there are no breakages or congestion in the conductor, great quantities of energy can flow through it. However, if there is a breakage or blockage in the energy conductor an explosion due to the damming up of forces is the result.

The human etheric organism is similar. If Mental, Astral or etheric bodies are in perfect harmony, and the individual is functioning through their chakra centres as directed by that person's soul, these energies from the higher worlds or causal body, even if they are of an insidious nature from the past, will have no effect on the person's physical body. The forces will be dissipated into the etheric body of the earth, for the person is naturally working with and clearing the taints of previous incarnations in a natural way. If there is emotional or physical injury to the base of spine, or base chakra, or any centre, a disease condition will begin, due to this accumulated energy with no-where to go.

Endocrine malfunction is a result of these dynamic forces that are hindered in their natural flow.

Radionics has the ability to work with these energies, remove the blockages and to cleanse the etheric body of the person and restore health.

Miasms can also be left behind after a clinically satisfactory and apparently complete recovery is made from an acute infection. These can be classed as toxins from childhood ailments perhaps, but still have a miasmic effect.

Dr George Lawrence in his works on Psionic Medicine refers to "retained toxins of acquired infection from earlier infectious illnesses, and that the elimination of this miasm whether hereditary or acquired sets going the restoration of the patient back to health." Dr Lawrence claimed that it was this unrecognisable factor which prevented the restoration of dynamic balance in a great many conditions that failed to respond to any form of treatment. According to him, the TK/TB miasms were primarily responsible in such conditions as asthma, eczemas, hay fever, sinusitis, migraine, and mental illness of various sorts; diabetes, Hodgkins disease and leukaemia also had their origins in these miasmic forces.

I am inclined to agree with Dr Lawrence, but would add that there must always be the factor to spark off or trigger the event of these illnesses. They can, if diagnosed in time, be successfully treated, or help given to the patient if it is their soul dictate that encourages the disease pattern to manifest.

The most common of the miasms found when analysing the subtle bodies are T.B., Syphilitic, Sycotic, Cancer and Psora. They may be found in the lower plane of the Mental body residing or functioning through the Base, Solar Plexus or Sacral Chakras, but mainly through the base chakra at a mental level.

The Practitioner can trace the origin of the miasms by using his radiesthetic sense, and dowsing in the causal body areas. It is of great assistance to know the origins of miasms and to establish how long the forces of the miasms are going to penetrate the lower self. It is often found that these forces of miasms are actually dammed up, or congested in a certain area and by treating other areas of the subtle body the forces are then allowed to flow and the miasm is eliminated out of the subtle body and into the etheric body of the earth, sometimes without any detrimental effect to the patient, but occasionally there is the healing crisis that manifests as the miasms dissipate. I belive this is what Hahnemann referred to as the "aggravation", as he then knew he had found the correct remedy.

It can therefore be said that miasms may be inherited from one's forefathers or from one's own previous incarnation, or they can be acquired during this lifetime from the etheric body of the earth, and miasms can cause predispositions to various types of illness. They very often have to be worked out by the patient's soul dictates via the energy centres of the body to the etheric of the earth. Miasms can also be acquired from infectious illness during this and other lifetimes.

Miasms may have no detrimental effects on people if the Mental, Astral and Physical etheric bodies are in total harmony and when the personality surrenders to the dictate of the soul, miasmic energies will have no disturbing effect on the physical body. The methods of treating the miasms will be dealt with in the chapter on the use of treatment instruments, and will show how energy flows from centre to centre and to the endocrine system of the physical body.

CHAPTER THREE

Energy Centres and Glands

"The centres determine man's point of evolution as far as his phenomenal expression is concerned; they work directly upon the physical body through the medium of the endocrine system."
Alice Bailey
Esoteric Healing

The process of ordered decent of the soul through successful graduations of subtle and physical matter and the full functions of all the chakra centres is adequately written up by Dr David Tansley in his book *Radionics and the Subtle Anatomy of Man*, and all practitioners of Radionics must study the work of Dr Tansley in detail. The book titles are given in the Bibliography at the end of this book.

For the sake of reference I will give the very basic details only of the chakra centres and the glands governed.

There are seven major chakra centres which are functioning at various levels in the Mental, Astral and physical etheric bodies. These centres develop as the soul incarnates into physical form and it is said that when the fine tubular threads of energy cross and recross twenty one times a major chakra centre develops. The reader must acqaint himself with the diagram on page 17 which shows these chakra centres and their relationships to one another, and how the incarnating soul's energies travel from one centre to another. This energy flow continues throughout a person's lifetime with the soul dictates and evolution of man expressing itself in this manner.

THE SEVEN MAJOR CENTRES, THEIR SITUATION, THE ALLIED GLAND AND THE AREA OF THE BODY GOVERNED ARE SHOWN BELOW.

THE CENTRE	SITUATION	ALLIED GLAND	AREA GOVERNED
The Crown	On the very top of the head.	Pineal Gland	Upper brain. Right eye.
The Ajna or Brow.	Between the eyes.	Pituitary	Lower brain, left eye, ears, nose, nervous system.
The Throat	Top of Back at Neck.	Thyroid	Bronchial and vocal apparatus, lungs and alimentary canal.
The Heart	Between Shoulder Blades.	Thymus	Heart, blood, vagus nerve, circulatory system.
The Solar Plexus	Above the waist.	Pancreas	Stomach, liver, gall bladder, nervous system.
The Sacral	Low down on spine, back.	Gonads	Reproductive system
The Base	Low down on spine at Apex of Sacrum.	Adrenals	Spinal column and kidneys.

There are, of course, many other minor centres which are used extensively by acupuncturists and pressure-point therapists. These points lie on meridians that run throughout the body, distributing energies that travel through the nervous system to all glands and organs.

Two other centres that are used extensively by Radionic practitioners are the Spleen centre and Alta Major.

CROWN CENTRE

Let us look at the centres again in order from the *Crown Centre*. This centre is located at the top of the head, and is often called the "Thousand Petalled Lotus"; it corresponds to the central spiritual sun. In man it is dynamic in quality and registers the purpose in life. The Crown Centre is now only slowly coming into development; it is not yet fully anchored in man (except that of the Master). The physical externalisation of the Crown centre is the Pineal Gland which is seated in between the left and right brain, governing the upper brain and the right eye. The intuition works through this centre and the connection with higher worlds when using the E.S.P. faculty; this is the dimension which is beyond our physical understanding of space and time.

The Ajna or Brow Centre, situated between the eyebrows, has its physical externalisation as the Pituitary Gland, and works on the lower or left brain, and controls the left eye, ears, nose and the nervous system. Logical and discriminate thinking emanates from this centre and it is the distribution of active intelligence.

The Pituitary Gland acts as a master controlling gland of the whole endocrine system. It manages the activities of the thyroid, parathyroid, gonads, adrenals, and pancreas.

The Throat Centre, located at the back of the neck manifests as the thyroid gland, with secondary expression as the parathyroid glands. These glands are essential to normal growth and control calcium and phosporus balance in the body. This centre is very much related to the Astral Body and the emotions, as emotional shock and trauma can cause this centre to react and promote many types of respiratory troubles, asthma being a very prevalent problem today, and it should be treated via the throat centre, with notice being taken of the Astral body condition as well.

The Heart Centre, found between the shoulder blades, corresponds to the heart of the sun and is the source of light and love. The heart centre registers the energy of love, and the dense physical externalisation is the thymus gland. This gland was thought by the medical profession to dry up and cease to function at puberty, but a lot more is now understood about the gland and its role in the hyperimmune or auto-immune reactions within the body.

The Solar Plexus Centre, situated below the diaphragm, is the seat of the emotions, and is very active in today's world.

The desires and emotions of the personality function through this centre and it is the outlet of the Astral Body into the outer world. The control of the centre is vital, or the personality will override soul dictates and conflict is the result; the desires must be transmitted into aspiration.

The externalisation of this centre is the Pancreas, also liver, gall bladder and the nervous system as related to the gastro-intestinal tract activities.

The Sacral Centre is located at the base of the lumbar spine, and has its physical externalisation as the gonads. This centre governs the whole of the reproductive system and guarantees the continuity of the human species. This centre has a close relationship with the throat chakra centre and it is often found that diseases or overstimulation of the sexual organs may be treated by directing energies to the throat centre, which draws the excessive energies up from the Sacral Centre.

The Base Centre is a vitally important centre and is situated at the apex of the sacrum, and its externalisation is the adrenal glands; it also governs the kidneys and the spinal column itself. This centre is the channel for the will to live, and anchors the body on the physical plane. It is relatively dormant in humanity today, but its activity is on the increase due to the stress and trauma of modern day living in this Western civilization.

It is from this base chakra centre at a mental level, that man begins his physical or low-self development, and this is why miasms or predispositions which are passed down from generation to generation, or assimilated from the etheric substance, can be treated most successfully in the base chakra.

The other two centres that are involved when working in Radionics are the Spleen and Alta Major.

The Spleen Centre is not situated on the spinal column but is the supplier of energy and vitality to all of the other major chakra centres. Prana or life energy from the sun manifests through this centre and any blockages of the spleen can cause lack of physical energy and lowered vitality to the other chakra centres.

The Spleen Centre is situated to the left and above navel at approximately waist level.

The Alta Major Chakra Centre is located at the base of the occiput and also governs the spinal column.

Its physical externalisation is the carotid gland. There is a direct relationship to the pituitary, base and heart chakra centres, being involved in the balance of tissue fluids, and the regulation of blood pressure. Analysis of Alta Major function is a good early warning and detection for impending heart conditions, as often patients that suffer so-called heart attacks have the true cause in the function of the Carotid Artery and Alta Major centre that controls the function of blood supply and blood pressure in the main artery from the heart to the head.

Returning to the seven major centres, it is interesting to note how they develop from the plane of the lower mind at incarnation, to the physical etheric body. For this purpose we must refer to the diagram shown on page 17 once again.

Note that the dividing line between the causal body and the low self is between the soul petals and the first chakra centres.

The first chakra centres to form when the soul begins its incarnation into physical form are the Base, Sacral and Solar Plexus Centres, the centres of digestion, excretion and procreation. These three centres derive their energies and vitality from the petals of sacrifice, knowledge and love in the soul, these being the totality of all information to build up the physical form via all the chakra centres as they develop in the Mental, Astral and etheric bodies.

The Mental Unit is the total blueprint of that person's life, its information emanating from the soul centre itself, and the spleen centre being the first centre to draw in the cosmic energy and distribute it to all other centres, not directly, but by flooding each of the bodies as they develop (see diagram 2).

We can therefore see that the incarnating soul as it builds the physical body of the foetus in the womb has already the information for the genetic coding, the will and life expression, and the digestive processes. Note that all these centres that develop initially in the plane of the lower mind are all below the diaphragm; they are the centres of the physical formations. It is only as the Astral Body comes into being that the Head, Throat and Heart Centres manifest; this is the life energy distribution all the way to physical form.

Not only does the foetus build a physical body based on these energy lines from centre to centre, but the whole of the person's life depends on this continued flow of energy. When blockages and deviations occur in these centres then disease manifests in the physical.

EGOIC LOTUS OF THE CAUSAL BODY

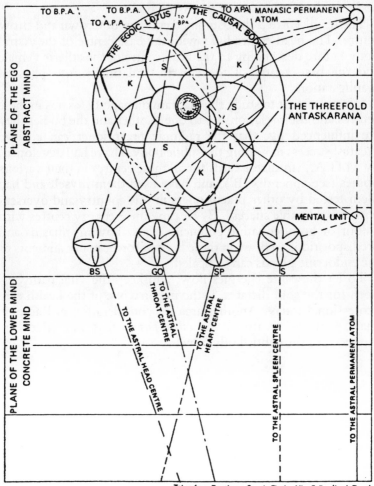

Taken from *Treatise on Cosmic Fire* by Alice Bailey (Lucis Trust)

A.P.A. = ATMIC PERMANENT ATOM
B.P.A. = BUDDHIC PERMANENT ATOM

K = KNOWLEDGE PETAL
L = LOVE PETAL
S = SACRIFICE PETAL

BS = BASE OF SPINE
GO = GENERATIVE ORGANS
SP = SOLAR PLEXUS
S = SPLEEN

Let us trace the path of the Base Centre in the lower mental body, to the head centre of the Astral body.

The head centre is the combined energies of Crown and Brow centre. The head centre links with the base centre of the Astral body before descending to the head centre of the etheric vehicle and the base centre of the etheric, and finally into physical manifestation.

It is important to study the diagram on page 17, as it is in these centres and their relationship to one another and the bodies they are influenced by, that the radionic practitioner can achieve greatest success in healing the subtle body. I have had developed, by M.G.A., simulator cards for all these centres in their various bodies (see appendix 'B'), and have used them myself and had them tested by other practitioners in this country and overseas with considerable success. By treating these energy centres with colour or homoeopathic potencies, thus allowing miasms and predispositions to flow on these lines of force, many ailments of the endocrine glands can be healed.

To let these life energies flow, and keep the vital pathways open for the soul dictates, is the major work of the health care professional today. Another area for consideration in Radionic analysis is the treatment of *other factors* that can affect the functions of the subtle body of man.

CHAPTER FOUR

Other Causative Factors

*"Never before did we know so much about disease and
pathological conditions — and so little about health and
wholeness".*

Dr Aubrey Westlake
The Pattern of Health

There are many causative and supplementary factors that
wreak havoc upon man, not only affecting his subtle anatomy
but the physical organism itself.

In this chapter I want to discuss the many factors which can be
treated and eliminated so that harmony and balance can be
restored within the body.

Our normal bodily functions are seriously interfered with by
various toxins, poisons and auto-intoxication.

First of these potent poisons are the chemical preservatives,
colouring and flavouring matter added to the food we eat, these
can be classed as catalase poisons, and affect almost all cells of the
body but do not affect certain bacteria.

Likewise there is the multitude of toxic agents used in farming
and agriculture, the insecticides, fungicides and weed killers.
There is the artifical stimulation of growth in animals and plants
by the use of hormones and anti-biotics, which interfere with the
respiratory enzymes of the cells and brings about the destruction
of catalase. Next we have to examine the use of alopathic drugs
and in particular the contraceptive pill. All the antidepressant
drugs that have devastating effects on the astral body. Still very
apparent today are the detrimental effects of vaccination, which I

will deal with in more detail later in this chapter.

Think of all the toxic gasses, fumes, the lack of oxygen and lack of exercise as we increase our dependence on labour saving devices. We have also the problem of man-made radiation from micro-wave ovens, X-rays, television radiation and many other forms of fall-out, all of which take their toll on man.

Man also has the problem of auto-intoxication from his teeth, tonsils and sleep.

As is obvious from the above mentioned factors, man is subjected continually to an interference with his vital enzyme functions and cellular metabolism, all of which is by inadvertence rather than intent.

It is important to establish in a Radionic Analysis if a patient is suffering from a degree of disturbance from factors such as poisons, toxins and auto-intoxication, and if so corrective measures may be taken to counteract the effects.

As I said earlier, some of the effects from factors induced long ago into the system remain for many years. In particular the detrimental effects of vaccination, or as is known to the Homoeopath, 'vaccinosis'. By vaccinosis we mean, as described by Dr J. Compton Burnett, the direct result of vaccination, plus the profound and often long lasting morbid constitutional state engendered by the vaccine virus. Burnett made the profound observation that the vaccine virus does not need to 'take' in order to produce the vaccinal dysrasia, and that many patients date the onset of ill-health from a so called unsuccessful vaccination. In other words a vaccination which never took. In Radionic Analysis many conditions of ill health have been found to emanate from the Detrimental effects of vaccination, including neuralgias of many kinds, skin disorders, indigestion and constipation, warts, growths and high blood pressure.

Dr J.H. Allen, in his work the "Chronic Miasm" talks of another mode of entrance of the sycotic poison into the organism, and that is through the vicious method of vaccination. Continued vaccination in years gone by has caused a great number of our race to be sycotic and our children bear the cross of their inherited miasms.

This vaccination of years gone by is the father of a multitude of skin diseases such as Erysipelas, Impetigo, Psoriasis, Marbella form rashes and Gangrene, also many types of Eczema, Dermatitis and Lupus Vulgaris.

Orthodox treatment today is purely suppressive and palliative whereas what the doctor is really faced with is a miasmic trait and stigmas passed on hereditarily. Further comment on this subject comes from Herbert A. Roberts, M.D. when he says "sycosis is the most degenerate of the miasms, in its suspicion, its quarrelsomeness, its tendency to harm others and to harm animals. It produces deceit, many forms of mania, and sycosis coupled with Psora is the basis of criminal insanity and suicide." Unless the miasm or stigmas are recognised, understood, and cured by homoeopathic or radionic means our patients cannot expect to gain optimum health.

Today orthodoxy is still pushing ahead with massive vaccination programmes, including the latest which is Whooping Cough, the effect of which may be felt in generations to come, just as we experience the effects of previous vaccination programmes today.

Homoeopathically these detrimental effects of vaccination can be helped by administering Thuja in potency ranges from 12c to 1M depending on the patient and the severity. Other Homoeopathic remedies such as Sulphur, Antimonium Tart, Mercurius, Phosphorus and Calc Carb have been found suitable. All these remedies have been found to be effective taken orally or given by Radionic projection.

The poisons and toxins previously mentioned, when established on a patient's analysis sheet as a causative factor, must be dealt with.

Obviously when a poison or toxin is established then it is pertinent to eliminate it from the diet or as much as possible from the patient's environment. But what of the established amounts within the system, how do we cope with them? Again this is where the Homoeopathic remedy comes into its own, by having the power to arouse within the patient the latent forces to expel the poison or toxin from the system. Patients must be warned of aggravation of symptoms or appearance of new symptoms as the body's vital forces eject the poisons from the living organism.

Similar effects are experienced when cleansing diets are administered, the body has a renewed chance of eliminating these toxic agents.

It is also possible to give a high potency of the poison or toxic agent to the patient in the form of a radionic projection or a simulation of toxic energy. This acts Homoeopathically as treating 'like with like'.

Rudolf Steiner speaks of "gradually accustoming a man to that which seems unsuitable to him, always strengthens his constitution." Therefore if you cannot administer the poisonous or toxic material homoeopathically, and it is a known foodstuff or allopathic drug that has caused the patient's ills, then wean them off slowly and treat the side effects or withdrawal symptoms with natural remedies and alternative diet.

Toxins that remain in the physical body can often be attributed to childhood illnesses, and it is important to check for the following: Measles toxins, Rubella, Whooping Cough, Mumps and even T.B. toxins.

It is also relevant to note that physical and etheric imbalances do not only arise from conventional infections, but can be produced by unsuspected influences from the environment which are inimicable to the human organism. The most important of these is the prevalent use of aluminium utensils both for cooking and in the preparation of processed foods.

This has a detrimental influence which does not arise from any chemical reaction within the body, but from the absorption by the food of certain energies in the aluminium which are incompatible with bodily harmony.

This form of aluminium poisoning or toxicity is not recognised by the orthodoxy, but its influence is widespread and often found as a major toxin when completing a radionic analysis.

There is a very interesting book named 'Divination of Disease', by Dr H. Tomlinson, wherein he maintains that aluminium poisoning or absorption causes imbalances of the ductless glands, and is responsible for a wide range of ailments including duodenal and gastric ulcers, liver and gall bladder complaints, rectal diseases and cancer, all of which are increasingly common today.

Prolonged absorption of aluminium and other noxious toxins such as Mercury and Silver from amalgam fillings in the teeth, have far reaching effects on the physical and etheric form. These many noxious influences in fact are the unsuspecting cause of many ills, some specific in symptoms, others merely resulting in a general lowering of vitality.

It is therefore evident that a person's health is influenced by a variety of miasms, residual toxins, some deep seated producing chronic illness, others less severe. The body is always striving for perfection and the innate intelligence endeavours to correct these imbalances and illness, the Radionic and Homoeopathic therapist has a powerful tool at hand in helping with the correction of disturbances in the underlying fabric of vital energy.

A further and important consideration is auto-intoxication of the body. The prime area being the oral cavity which is the subject of the next chapter. The oral cavity not only acts as the channel for ingesting poisons and toxins but the teeth and tonsils can toxify the body continuously but inadvertently.

One other little known area of autointoxicant is sleep.

To expand on this I will quote from Rudolf Steiner's *Spiritual Science and Medicine.*

"All the activities whose trend is to force the processes of the lower organic sphere of mankind into the upper, are enhanced during sleep. It is necessary to take great care in describing sleep. Sleep is indeed one of the best remedies but only if employed to the right amount, neither too much or too little, so that it suits the particular human individuality. Too much sleep i.e. more sleep than the individual in question can sustain, is not curative but toxic. During a too long spell of sleep, the internal barrier lets through a continuous infiltration; too much passes through from the first digestive area into the region of blood and lymph formation. Man is exposed to this danger quite generally: the lower organic sphere is in a permanent state of sleep, so man is always in danger of harmful effects on the blood through the processes of the lower organic sphere."

What Steiner is saying, is that the mundane process of digestion below diaphragm and all the energies and forces that control those processes, are able to influence the Subtle body areas above diaphragm during sleep.

This of course, is a natural process of evolution that man

during his lifetime should endeavour to raise the energies from below to above the diaphragm into the Heart and Head centres. During sleep the Astral body and above diaphragm chakra centres relax control of the body and the energies of the lower forces predominate. Many know too well the toxic effects of the hangover feeling from the long sleep, perhaps induced by the extra one-for-the-road, but ending up with more sleep induced toxins than alcoholic.

One other aspect of auto-intoxication is scar tissue. Scars when tender cause inflammation below the surface. Toxins flow into the bloodstream, and energy from scar tissue can travel along meridians of the body, and with this in mind one should know that scar tissue has memory.

Further lesions in that area release toxic effects into the bloodstream and meridians only to accumulate and expand into pathological symptoms.

CHAPTER FIVE

Auto-Intoxication and the Oral Cavity

"Any medical subject under discussion today has, as its background, those initial studies in anatomy, physiology and general biology, which are the preliminaries to medicine proper. These preliminaries bias the medical mind in a certain direction from the first; and it is absolutely essential that such bias should be rectified."

Rudolf Steiner ,
Spiritual Science and Medicine.

It is of vital importance that as Radionic Practitioners we continue to develop not only our tools of analysis and treatment, but also systems and procedures useful in the field of preventative medicine.

The present day hospital is a place of disease end-results and not perhaps the best place for research. This work might more profitably be done at the opposite end of the scale, the healthier end, in this field of preventative medicine.

Our bodies have many ways of indicating the present state of health, as demonstrated in Iridology, Reflexology, Cranial Analysis, Applied Kinesiology, the palms of the hands etc. One area that has so far attracted little notice is the Oral Cavity and its associated auto-intoxication. It is through the oral and nasal cavities, that we ingest all the nutrients for life support, as well as the toxins and poisons from our environment. The breath of life that supports us passes across the lymphatic protection areas known as the tonsils and adenoids. These glands can also be a focus of inflammation and infection even after the successful

Tonsilectomy and Adenoidectomy. The remainting stubs can be the source of Streptococcus or Staphyloccus infections that continually pollute the blood-stream, and cause irritation of the meridian energy that passes through the stubs. This pollution not only causes Toxaemia but such conditions as Colitis, joint inflammation and many skin symptoms related to blood poisoning.

Radionic analysis can pin-point the focus of inflammation, which can be treated with the necessary cards or rates for the condition. Corresponding organs can also be irritated by these imbalances and focuses of inflammation. Homoeopathic simulated remedies and nosodes offer a wide range of therapeutic treatment in these areas. Radiesthetically I have found very interesting links when checking auto-intoxication of the tonsils and adenoids. These areas are also linked to organs within the body and certain corresponding teeth. These links can be verified when reading some basic literature on Acupuncture as well as the work of Dr Voll and Electo-Acupuncture techniques. It is essential when conducting a Radionic Analysis to check for auto-intoxication, particularly from the teeth and tonsils. It is often found that diseased conditions of internal organs have their causes in a tonsular focus or an offending tooth.

I have found the following link-up apparent for tonsils, sinuses and related organs.

TONSILS	SINUSES	ORGANS
Laryngeal	Maxillary	Stomach – Solar Plexus
Tubule	Ethmoidal	Large Intestine – Lungs
Pharyngeal	Frontal	Bladder – Kidney
Palatine	Sphenoidal	Gall-Bladder – Liver
Lingual	Middle Ear	Small Intestine – Heart

The emphasis of society today is towards conservation of the teeth at all costs, and the dental surgeon is faced with pressing demands to salvage teeth which have already been attacked by decay and disease. Overlooked are the links with the rest of the body and the process of man's evolution, particularly during formative years of the younger generation. Rudolf Steiner tells us that every organ of man has a two fold task: one related to an orientation to consciousness; the other its opposite, to an orientation to the purely organic process. Alice Bailey also tells us that as man evolves his consciousness and advances along the spiritual path he will experience problems related to the teeth and ears. The recognition of these facts has so far been neglected in the study of the teeth. From the orthodox and materialistic point of view, the teeth are more or less regarded as mere chewing implements, but they are more than that. Their dual nature is easily apparent. For if teeth are tested chemically they appear to be part of the bone system, but ontogenetically they emerge from the skin system. The teeth are not only implements for chewing but are also very essential implements for absorption. Teeth have a mechanical external action and an extremely fine, spiritualised absorbative action.

In formative years teeth take in Fluorine, and if deprived man becomes too clever! The Fluorine input restores the necessary amount of mental dullness which we need if we are to be balanced human beings, we require this constant minute dosage for protection against mental hyper-activity. The premature decay of teeth allows man to control naturally the certain point of awareness or cleverness that he should not go beyond.

Man as it were, disintegrates his teeth so that the fluorine action should not go beyond a certain point and make him dull. The interaction of cause and effect are very subtle here! Under certain circumstances we have need of the action of fluorine, in order not to become too clever. But we can injure ourselves by excess in this respect, and then our organic activity destroys and decays the teeth. Just think what is happening to the younger generation today with the salvage of teeth, fluoridation of the water supply and toothpaste. What of the energy connections between teeth and the corresponding organs of the body?

What too, of the heavy metal poisons used in amalgam filling materials that pollute the body? This material being used simply as an end to preserving teeth that the individual wants to eject from his system. A further problem I have pin-pointed using Radionic Analysis, and had confirmed by orthodox dentistry, is the vagrant buccal currents that form from dental filling materials and other metals in the mouth. Dental materials can create a battery-like effect in the mouth that through meridian irritation can incite chronic pain syndromes, dermatological lesions and disturbance of the gastro-intestinal tract. Metals in the mouth decompose through the process of electrolysis and materials used in the compounds pollute the body. These metals of differing composition, when adjacent in the mouth, set up minute electric currents between the tooth, the gingival and the buccal membranes of the cheek. Slow electrolytic dispersion of amalgam tooth substances will cause sensitisation, in addition the 'mouth battery' effect; electric currents between various metals in and on the teeth, cause irritation of the nervous system. Many previously therapy-resistant conditions will respond to the removal of old amalgam fillings and replacement with porcelain or other plastic compounds. Radionic Analysis is a simple, yet effective method of detecting the toxic metal that is inimicable to the body systems. The Mercury used in amalgam dental fillings acts as a solvent for the other metals used. Dental amalgams may contain silver, tin, zinc and copper, and the Radionic Analysis should check for auto-intoxication and the detrimental effects of these metals when a dental focus has been established. When dispersion of amalgam fillings takes place due to the electrolytic process or mouth battery effect, Mercury, being a severe poison, will provoke pathological symptoms, however minute these traces of Mercury may be. I have found in patients many symptoms that have cleared by treating the teeth. Among these symptoms, the following were direct results of dental or oral cavity sensitisation:

Depressions, Gastro-enteritis, various intestinal irregularities, Dermatitis, Urticaria, Eczema, Headaches and Respiratory Disorders.

Removal of Amalgam fillings in corresponding teeth resulted in permanent cures of the above mentioned disorders.

Not only does the Amalgam dissolvement cause problems, but also the electrical currents in the mouth that are caused by Amalgam next to gold, bridges in the mouth, and the metallic bands so popular today with Orthodontists in correcting tooth alignment in the younger generation. Cappings and root canals also play their part in converting the oral cavity into a mouth battery and centres of inflammatory focus. I have met many holistic Dental Surgeons that use a combination of the Rae Analyser and the Triplet Instruments along with the Dr Voll Dermatron using the principle of electro-acupuncture. The Rae system of treatment using the triplet instrument can direct healing and correction influence to the offending tooth and organ system. This has resulted in cures for patients that had consulted doctor after doctor without success. It has always amazed me that Dental Surgeons with the holistic approach examine their patients on the chiropractic couch and take a full physical case history before looking in the mouth, whereas the G.P. in this country when taking a physical case history usually shows no interest at all in the oral cavity. Medical opinion on the importance of electric current formation in the mouth is diverse. Medical students in today's universities hear very little or nothing at all about the mouth battery and resultant poisons by heavy metals, and it is largely disregarded in the daily practice of medicine.

The following oral symptoms may be attributed to the buccal current formations:

Lingual burning sensations, apthae, dryness in the mouth, Hypertrophic Gingivitis and the common Metallic taste in the mouth.

Irritations of the nervous system and the psyche may appear as a side effect to oral current formations.

I find it very important to check any degrees of deviation in the oral cavity when conducting the Radionic Analysis, and any patient that displays severe organ disfunction or any other previously mentioned symptoms, I always check for oral cavity or teeth problems. I also check the corresponding teeth with the organ systems, skeletal system, etc, even endocrine glands are all related to certain teeth.

If there is Amalgam poisoning, I would use the Homoeopathic simulated remedy first. If this fails restoration of the filling is essential, or complete removal of the tooth. Radionically one can establish if the tooth is going to respond, if the tooth is even necessary and if the nosode, Radionic projection or serially diluted remedy will be successful.

The following list gives further symptoms that can be a direct result from Amalgam poisoning in the oral cavity.

PRIMARY SYMPTOMS FROM AMALGAM POISIONING

Headaches	Intestinal Disorders
Facial Neuralgia	Psychic Disturbances
Migraines	Vegetative Disturbance
Dizziness	Dermal Disorders
Insomnia	Rheumatic Symptoms
Tinnitus	Bronchial Asthma
Nausea	Depression
Cardiovascular Disorders	Gastrointestinal Disorders

PRIMARY SYMPTOMS RELEVANT TO ELECTRICAL CURRENTS

Headaches	Migraines
Dizziness	Vegetative Disturbance
Lingual Burning	Dryness of the Mouth
Gingivitus	Metallic Taste
Hypochondria	Cervical Spine Syndrome

To understand dental disease it is necessary to examine not only the relationship between the tooth and the organ, but the person and his environment. Also important is the recognition of the stages of man's evolvement on the spiritual path, and the relationship between the physical person and the vital essence. If this can be done, the dental practice takes on a very different meaning, a new dimension is added. In the oral cavity we are looking at yet another area of our physical anatomy that displays information to us in the form of causative factors in disease. Holistic dentistry is already a recognised field of research and practice in the U.S.A. and some parts of the Continent. Radionic Practitioners will therefore find an increasing need to inform the dental profession of their importance in diagnosis and treatment of physical anomalies, and not just as inspectors and repairmen of the oral cavity. Radionics again shows how it can benefit our patients as well as complementing the work of other health care professionals in the development of preventative medicine techniques and research into chronic disease syndromes.

CHAPTER SIX

Essential Simplicity:
The Homoeopathic Connection

"The economy of the Universe is based upon Essential Simplicity, and as such gives us symbols that reflect this simplicity."

Malcolm Rae
1976

In previous chapters, I have dealt with the origins of man, the etheric body, the energy centres and it is now time to discuss how in Radionic Analysis we observe the condition of the physical body.

We are aware that the physical structure is purely the material evidence from the blue print of etheric patterns and energy centres. As such it reflects the harmonies and disharmonies apparent in the subtle body in the form of disease. Therefore it is unnecessary to analyse in great detail disease symptoms and pathological conditions as treatment will only be totally successful if applied to that subtle organising energy, i.e. the causative areas.

Orthodox approaches of specialising and compartmentalising of the human body is getting further and further away from true causes. Symptoms are effects from causes, and it is only necessary to establish degrees of deviation in the physical structure based on organ functions and glandular secretions. These organ and glandular functions have their etheric counterparts, and the completed analysis will show these correspondences.

This book is based on the work of the late Malcolm Rae and as such will deal mostly in the use of the Analyser and Treatment instruments designed by him.

The principles of the card system and its origins are adequately detailed in the book *Dimensions of Radionics*, by David Tansley in collaboration with Malcolm Rae. At this point however, I will recap on a few basic fundamentals that Practitioners must be cognisant of, if the system of cards and instruments is to be utilized to the full.

It is important that the Practitioner understands how his right brain function, utilizing the external visualisation of the pendulum, receives the correct answers when questioning the condition of the patient. Left brain logic must be satisfied by symbolic representation either by correct thought, drawn pattern or symbol, before the right brain will receive the correct information. Whether this information is in regard to the patient or the universe itself, and whether an instrument is used or purely the Radiesthetic faculty. Clarification and intent is of prime importance when posing questions for the intuition and radiesthetic senses.

At this point it is relevant to discuss certain points raised by Malcolm Rae in his notes dated around 1976.

(a)   The activity of thinking does not produce vibrations but selects vibrations from a wide spectrum source, but does give the apparency of producing them. The nature of the vibrations selected is directly related to the nature of the thought and not to the intensity of it.

(b)   Identical thoughts in different individuals select identical frequencies of vibration from the source within the universe.

(c)   The intensity of a thought is not the direct result of mental activity and cannot be influenced by it, but it can sometimes be influenced by emotional activity.

To interject here, one can see that analysis and treatment should only be carried out when the Practitioner is in a balanced state emotionally, and that the time spent on one particular thought is not proportional to the amount of information received. A lengthy period of time spent thinking about one particular aspect of an analysis will not reveal any further information than that which first comes to mind, based on the question posed.

We can see how this link up with patient, practitioner and symbols of thought patterns, create a triangulation when using the analysis or treatment instruments. We have visually in front of us the symbol of the thought patterns for the location for which we are seeking information (i.e. the location). We have the patient's witness and ourselves the enquirer with the externalisation being the pendulum.

When a patient with a genuine intent for healing thinks of approaching the practitioner for help, a thought from their free will selects from the universal source an existing thought pattern, and likewise the healer selects from the same universal source, thought patterns when seeking causes of that patient's ills. The witness sent by the patient, whether it be hair, blood or photograph is the patient's symbol of intent to be healed.

Briefly one can say as follows:

(a)   Analysis and treatment thoughts select the necessary vibrations from a wide spectrum source within the universe.

(b)   The nature of the vibration is directly related to the nature of the thought, hence thought patterns can be represented by numerical rates or symbols on cards in the form of radii.

(c)   If the nature of the free thought in asking for healing draws on the universal source, the healer will draw on the same universal source to enact the healing using the same vibration. The 'asking vibration' by patients are mirrored by the 'helping vibrations' of the healer.

(d)   You cannot implant a thought in another persons mind unless the pattern of that thought already existed.

Could the foregoing statements be a clue to the efficacy of compensating rates when using dial sets, or the mirror image or high potency projections of the card symbols to the patient? Here we have a direct link with the Homoeopathic potency. If cards used in a Rae simulator to potentise material for oral use can cause a healing in a patient homoeopathically speaking, and cards used in the same instrument when projected to the patient at a distance using the interrupter and the patient's witness also cause a healing, could there then be a similarity between Homoeopathy and Radionics?

What we are using in classical Homoeopathy is a potency, or proportions of thought forms that created matter used in the succession dilution process in preparing that remedy.

Let us recap and examine a few basic concepts that have been discussed so far, as well as some theories I wish to put forward on the concept of Homoeopathy, thought forms and basic simplicity.

Every individual is a 'unique' integration of 'essence' and 'substance' (or if the reader prefers it of 'non material' and of 'material components'), and the essential simplicity operates his physical body by a process of energising via the subtle bodies and chakra centres. This energising occurs as and when required. Sets of thought patterns operate to cause corrective bodily action to compensate for the continued environmental changes.

As long as the process can compensate completely for the changes, and do it rapidly enough, the individual will remain healthy, and will not be aware of the process taking place.

The process was, in fact, designed to function without impinging upon awareness, and one is not normally aware of changes in depth of breathing, pulse rate or release of blood sugar.

In health, one becomes aware of some of these factors, but only when operating close to one's limitations of tolerance. Such an example can be extremes of temperature or humidity, or when driving one's body to near maximum capabilities, as in very strenuous unaccustomed exertion, and since it must be assumed that the repertoire of thought patterns that direct a healthy body into life are in accordance with the designed purpose of that body, the invasion by the unconscious processes into consciousness is no more than a sensible warning.

These warnings can be pain, tiredness or spasm. Many are the symptoms that patients display in this warning process, telling us all is not well. Ignoring these warnings or minor symptoms can result in permanent damage or disease.

But the penalty of ambition, greed and living up with society is that many of the purely physically ideal requirements are made subservient to the individual's ambitions and social needs. Man very often transgresses the laws of nature. He misses regular meals and sleep, drinks when it is socially appropriate rather than when his body requires liquid, and in short generally overrides the endeavours of the 'Essential Simplicity' to conduct his body efficiently, whenever he finds it more expedient so to do.

Not only this, but when the clamour of the 'Essential Simplicity' to help by means of conscious change of attitude, or activity becomes too insistent, he uses alopathic drugs to negate or reduce the clamour.

Thus man converts the wonderful thought patterns and natural boundaries with which he was born, and through which his creator intended his energies to flow freely, productively and without artificial impedance, into patterns of barriers which not only restrict his available energy but also generate stress, but when energised by the 'Essential Simplicity' will yield inappropriate instructions to the body.

Thought patterns and symbols depicted on cards are the most likely system to convert a barrier-stress system into a boundary-energy system, because a geometric representation of such a thought pattern can be energised, and the thought pattern itself replicated. It can be introduced into an individual in many ways (with permission and due intent) and will go far towards restoring his original boundary-energy systems, and thus improve health and happiness.

Let us take this concept of the thought-patterns and 'Essential Simplicity' a step further and endeavour to construct a connection with the Homoeopathic Potency. If we can rightly assume that we mortals are a product of the Creator, or the universal mind, along with the rest of creation, then we can fairly assume that we are the products of thought patterns. Universal thought patterns that emanate from within the universal source.

Just as we perceive colour emanating from crystals, or we measure vibrations from a bar magnet, we should consider initially what produced the crystal and the material of the magnet.

If universal thought patterns had some part to play in the formation of crystals and the magnet, we should consider if the emanations and colours from the crystal we perceive are from within emanating out, or from outside emanating in, that materialises matter, these emanations must be part of, or the carriers of the constructive patterns that create matter. Let us mention again Malcolm Rae's recorded statement of the late 1970's, which is relevant at this stage of our discussions "Man does not produce, or the act of thinking does not produce thought vibrations, but selects thought vibrations from within the universal source."

Therefore man in his daily activity responds to, and selects existing thought patterns that are within the universe, and will subconsciously select patterns or proportions of patterns that will heal or restore the boundary-energy relationship.

The healer or Homoeopathic Practitioner will do the same for his patient when using his intuition in questioning the universal source for his selection of the correct Homoeopathic remedy.

If all matter of the plant, animal and mineral kingdoms are a product of the universal source, then all homoeopathic remedies whether made by the M.G.A. process or traditional succession and dilution fall under the same analogy. We can now fairly state that a Homoeopathic potency is in fact a proportion of a thought pattern from within the universal source, whether that remedy was made from the mother tincture of a plant, animal or mineral source.

We can also state that the succession and dilution from mother tincture is purely a process of producing a proportion or 'potency' of the original thought pattern, by splitting or proportioning the atomic or energy structure stage by stage. We know in homoeopathic teachings that the higher the dilution the more powerful the remedy becomes, as the approach is made by the continual proportioning to the source of the pattern within the universe. There is no measurable material substance at all in a potency of above 23x or 12c, it is pure energy or that proportion of the original thought pattern that created the matter initially. We know that the M.G.A. system of Homoeopathic simulation is proven beyond doubt, tried and tested by hundreds of Homoeopaths since its establishment by Malcolm Rae in the late 1960's. We know that Geometric expression of Radii on cards within the circle represents the thought pattern of a substance based upon that universal principle.

A potency or proportion of that pattern will influence the thought patterns of the human organism, as we are all emanations from the universal source, man, animal, plant and mineral kingdoms. It is the selection of the correct potency or proportion which is of paramount importance because homoeopathic potencies act at levels before matter is created, that is why a remedy with no material content can influence and heal the physical body of man, it acts to restore the boundaries and energies, or as the Homoeopathic teaching states, the vital essence "it is all essential simplicity."

CHAPTER SEVEN

Essential Simplicity:
The Radionic Connection

"As the etheric body pervades – to use the word – the whole of the physical organism of man, it is obvious that if one uses the proprioceptive nervous system to tune in – so to speak – to the etheric body in its mentation aspect, complete and detailed knowledge of all and every aspect of the physical-etheric structure and function of man is available, as well as the adjustments produced by the astral forces and the forces of ego. This I now think is exactly what Radiesthetic faculty is and the way it works."

Dr Aubrey Westlake
Life Threatened

Returning now to our Radionic work, we know that information for the analysis and the healing vibrations to our patients travels on thought waves. Once the link has been made between patient and practitioner and the vibration of the thoughts are linked, only then can the varying detailed information be obtained by the practitioner. The carrier or thought wave, like that of a radio station remains unaltered by the information it bears.

The true intent of the practitioner is of paramount importance. There are some schools of thought that consider detrimental influence or inducement of the disease being checked upon is placed upon a person when rates or cards are placed on an instrument with the hair sample when doing an analysis and inadvertently left on for a period of time. This is all in the mind of these practitioners and is an absurdity; they must seek to clarify between their left brain logic and their right brain intent.

Getting back to the physical structures in the radionic analysis we may fairly state that the whole point of using an instrument lies in the fact that by placing rates on a dial, or using a card with partial radii to represent the disease or part of the body, you have a symbol or value for the disease or part of the body which you are investigating. This saves the practitioner from trying to keep his thoughts on the factor whilst at the same time seeking the information which travels on that thought wave which is giving him the causes or degrees of imbalance of that part of the body.

In terms of basic simplicity the structures have been broken down into areas of the body and functions that correspond to the energy centres or chakras. Study of the subtle analysis chart on page 00 shows that subtle body locations are placed on the right hand side in order of Mental, Astral, Etheric and nadis and physical structures are listed in a certain order on the left hand side, beginning with Aural system, Visual system and C.N.S., all the way down to Teeth and Tonsils.

This corresponds with the right hand side of the chart as Aural and Visual are reflected in the state of the Brow and Ajna Chakra centres. Teeth and tonsils can reflect auto-intoxication factors. "Degrees of deviation from functional perfection" are measured for each structure, as well as the second question. "What is the degree at worst point?"

The reason for asking the second question is, for example the mean or average degree of deviation in the Aural system may be 30°, but the degree at worst point may be 70°. This would indicate an infection or inflammatory matrix that is causing a high degree at worst point but not affecting the average or mean function of the aural system in general. We would have in this case perhaps an inner ear infection such as Otitis Media that was a deviation or intensity of disease causing a 70° deviation from norm, but not affecting the overall function of the patient's hearing ability.

Before going onto the next chapter of describing the procedures used in the Radionic Analysis I wish to put over an aspect of the analysis that I have practised for many years. It has been used by many other practitioners and I have had it confirmed as a reasonable method of questioning when beginning the analysis.

The reason for the following additional questioning was as follows. After treating patients at the root causes, they would improve for a period of time and then the symptoms would return. I wanted to know why this happened, and so investigated the matter fully. The following question when posed for subtle anatomy analysis gives us answer. "What is the degree of deviation from the causal body affecting the optimum function of . . ." This gave a different reading in degrees of deviation, from the normal question of "What is the degree of deviation from functional perfection?"

As an example, what I was getting was this:
(a) A degree of deviation measuring $60°$ from functional perfection of the Mental Body.
(b) But a reading of $0°$ from the causal body affecting the optimum function of the mental body.

The detrimental affect caused was a necessity for the patient at that particular time in his life. No degree of deviation from causal means that there is a causative factor travelling on the energies of the causal rays that affects the mental body or whatever etheric body is being analysed. It is right then for that patient to be affected by a karmic influence from the causal body.

This type of information lets you know at the outset of the analysis that the causes are either from the causal body or from the patient's own environment or low self, and that your treatment will be more fully effective if it is directed at low self or environmental, or purely help to the patient in coping with problems if it is from the causal body.

These influences or disturbances that travel via the causal are predispositions or even miasms that can emanate from the soul dictates, and should not be confused with the totality of the causal rays which directs the person in the way of life, i.e. glamour, virtues and vices.

Again we have the analogy that the carrier wave has certain static vibrations in the form of virtues, vices and glamour, but can also carry predispositions and miasms of varying natures that cause havoc in the low self. We can treat the patient below the soul dictates in the plane of the lower mind, but not in the causal body or free will area. We can however analyse the causal body, for our thoughts can penetrate and link with the vibrations and patterns on these carrier waves. These are the processes that give us the factors and symptoms that are causing the degrees of deviation in the subtle bodies and the physical structures. This is the Radionic analysis, the bridge between two worlds, it is also the point where the treatment takes place, as often in practice the healing takes place at the time of the analysis.

This is not to say that only one treatment is necessary at time of analysis, for it must be stressed that going through a ritual of treating a patient radionically on a daily basis is unnecessary.

Many Practitioners of Radionics combine a procedure of one or two radionic projections of a specialised nature, perhaps weekly, with the group treatment instrument on a four hourly basis, and their patients participation being the taking of oral homoeopathic remedies, biochemics or vitamins.

This in my opinion is a balanced healing programme and does have the desired healing effects.

It is of vital importance that the patient participates in the healing. The patient has initiated the healing intent by approaching the practitioner originally, but it is important to keep the patient's motivation going by administering some form of oral remedy. I do not believe the patient should be told to sit back and just let the radionic practitioner do the work, this lacks incentive from both sides.

We can see then that a radionic analysis can be described as a procedure using symbols and rituals. The symbol of the practitioner are his cards, rates, instruments and the pendulum. The ritual is the systematic measuring of those parts of the subtle body and physical anatomy as laid out on the case history sheet.

The symbol from the patient is the hair sample or bloodspot and his ritual is perhaps the taking of an oral remedy on a repetitive basis, or reporting regularly on his condition.

Care should be taken to ensure that only cards purchased from Magneto Geometric Applications are used in the instruments. There are no agents or other suppliers and are only available from the London address shown at the end of this book. The cards are distinguishable by the name "Malcolm Rae" on the front and by either of the two addresses or the MGA logo on the reverse as shown below.

MALCOLM RAE.
47. Lee High Road.
Lewisham.
London. SE13 5NS.
England.

Telephone: 01 · 852 8292

MAGNETO
GEOMETRIC
APPLICATIONS

Malcolm Rae
3 The Hermitage
Westwood Park
Forest Hill
London SE23 3RU
England

Tel: 01-699 6604

The M.G.A. cards for use in the Radionic instruments are designed in the same manner as any of the homoeopathic cards. Cards are available for all known subtle body locations, chakras, acupuncture points and meridians, all physical organs, symptoms and locations, as well as known physical conditions and diseases.

The date for M.G.A. cards is obtained radiesthetically using the constant formula: "The ascending series of angles each expressing to the nearest whole degree of arc between the vertical radius representing no degrees from the centre of the potency simulator diagram, which solely represents .... (name of remedy or location) in such a way that a perfect potency of it may be prepared in the potency simulator for which it is designed."

To this formula, expressed as a symbol, the brain will respond in the same way as it responds to other symbols which instruct it how to think about a given subject, as for example a '$' sign, which tells the reader how to regard the numeral which follows it. When the reader sees '$5' he will hardly be aware of the '$' sign, which nevertheless controls the context in which he considers the '5'.

Informative symbols of this type can be described as 'operators' and the formula for finding the data of simulator cards has been crystalised into an operator to ensure that whilst dowsing for the cards data, the dowsers thoughts are influenced only by the precise definition of the data he requires.

Data having been obtained, a master card is drawn, using the degree marks of a much larger circle than those printed on the production cards in order to produce greater accuracy. The production cards are then produced from the master card, the whole system now having been computerised. Each card may require up to 6 partial radii, and it is interesting to note that combinations of 6 radii drawn to an accuracy of 1 degree of arc, amount to 467,916,713,911,200 – so there is no likelihood of shortage of representation space.

The importance of the radii and their position within the 360 degrees is paramount, and it is the relationship or degree of arc between one radii and another which is of significance.

Many enquirers have searched for an explanation as to how the card and its partial radii can, when encircled by a circular magnet produce a vibration that can be recorded by water. Malcolm Rae's own experience and explanation of how water can record and hold vibratory patterns has been detailed in the book "Dimensions of Radionics."

The important fact here is that the magnet produces the carrier wave and the geometric expression or universal relationship between radii which is the universal thought pattern on the card, travels on that magnetic carrier wave. It is not so much the magnetic vibrations travelling down the partial radii on the card that cause interference patterns, but the position of radii to one another within the circle, as Tad Mann explained when he investigated the card system.

Tad Mann, writer of the *Round Art*, shows us how a radii in a certain position within the circle and its relationship with the next radii is equivalent to the microcosm within the macroscosm. The radii are relative to planet positions within the 360 degrees of the universe, and so influence man and all creations on the earth. The whole birth pattern or birth chart of a person can be put down within a circle with influences being shown as partial radii relative to planet position at birth.

This concept was taken one step further by Tad Man when he explained how he had placed radii on a card relative to a patients ills, that is by dividing the 360 degrees into 12 segments and drawing radii based on his knowledge of astrology. Within the first 30° of Aries when there were head symptoms, and likewise by placing a radii with 30° of Taurus for throat symptoms and so forth.

A patient displaying symptoms of head pains, sore throat, infection of the blood and perhaps aches and pains of the knee joints, should have 4 radii positioned on a card as for diagram shown below.

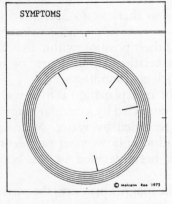
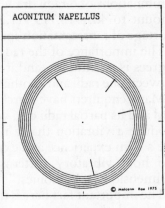

CARD A　　　　　　　　　　　　　　**CARD B**

Likewise, the card for Acnonite, which of course was dowsed from the thought concept of the original mother tincture has radii in the same positions.

This surely means that a relationship exists mathematically or geometrically speaking between radii position for the disease and the cure, because card A represents the relative points astrologically of bodily areas of man affected by universal knowledge and planetary influence, and card B represents the same universal knowledge that can heal the patient with symptoms such as head pains, sore throats etc. Astrologically this proves the cards to be symbols of thought forms they represent.

It remains for the healer to select the correct potency or proportion of that healing symbol.

These card symbols when placed in an instrument allow us to dowse the degrees of deviation of the organ or system, the pendulum will register the correct degree of deviation, based on the question posed.

We know the card symbol is a universal truth, therefore we need not doubt the answer or pendulum response.

The ability to measure degrees of deviation allows us to record and monitor our patients progress, as well as selecting the correct remedy for treatment. The system now used in the preparation of homoeopathic remedies by simulation techniques has come a long way since Ruth Drown devised her method for making homoeopathic remedies by subjecting them to various rates or numerical variations on dials on her HOMO-VIBRA-RAY instruments.

What Ruth Drown was doing was selecting proportions or variations between numbers and subjecting the Sac.Lac to the interference pattern created, she was very cognisant of the universal geometric patterns of thought forms which we use in our daily practice.

What actually happens when we administer a high potency of a homoeopathic remedy or give a radionic projection of a potency from a card representing a universal thought pattern, is, we expand the tolerance of the situations which the patient is experiencing, we increase the energy and restore the boundaries.

CHAPTER EIGHT

The Pendulum Trainer

*"If one wishes to communicate with a superior level it is first
necessary to acknowledge that a higher level exists."*
J.H. Reyner
Psionic Medicine

There is a wealth of literature on extra-sensory phenomena and
detailed discussion here would be inappropriate. It is however,
important for all students learning the use of the pendulum to
fully understand what is happening and why certain reactions
occur. The most common type of pendulum used with Radionic
instrumentation is as shown on page 67 and is of a conical shape
manufactured from clear resin, containing a seven coil wire spiral
which has been wound based on the Golden Mean ratio. It is
best used with a short string of approximately 6″ length; tie a few
knots down its length in order to make the holding of the string
easier.

Pendulum reaction comes about by the posing of vital and
correct questions to a universal problem, whether it be yourself,
a patient or the universe itself. When posing questions using the
pendulum, always induce life with a gentle swing, do not let it
hang motionless. It is part of you and your vital senses, just as
your eyes will only function when bathed in light, your
pendulum will only function when energised. The conversion of
the movement into a positive or negative giration will only come
about when the correct question has been posed and accepted by
the left brain logic, which in turn activates the right brain
communication with the higher levels and the correct answer

returns to the left brain immediately, and the neuro-muscular reaction will cause the pendulum to swing either clockwise or anti-clockwise. A straightforward swing similar to that which was initiated indicates that the response is neutral, or the question needs reformulating.

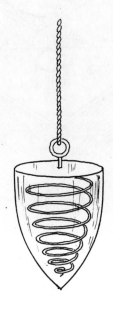

The Pendulum

The best method I have found in training students is the use of the Malcolm Rae Pendulum trainer, as illustrated below.

PENDULUM TRAINER

1. The instrument is depicted by the following sketch:

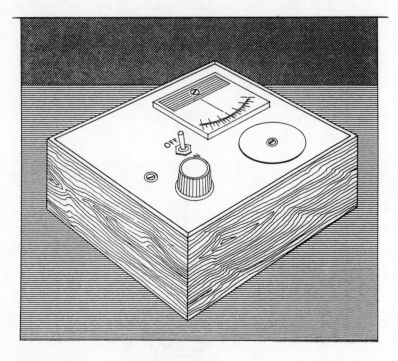

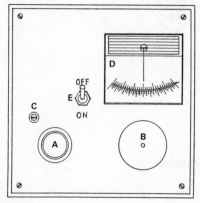

A Control Knob

B Chromium-plated Disc

C Screw Head

D Meter

E On/Off Switch

The Pendulum Training Instrument

What is helpful when training with this instrument is that it enables the students to understand a pendulum reaction in measuring degrees, as the meter scale is laid out in degrees similar to that of the Analyser board.

Pendulum reaction and accuracy is obtained by practice and the understanding that we are questioning the universal mind based on symbols and rituals. In a Radionic Analysis you will find that your pendulum reaction will be fast and accurate when you understand the symbol of intent from the patient's (witness) is on your instrument, and your own symbol of the area being questioned is in the form of card with a geometric expression of that area is located within the instrument. When a question is posed of the patient the link is established between the right brain functions of the practitioner and patient in one instantaneous reaction, the answer is then relayed via the neuro-muscular responses to the finger tips and the reaction is noted by the pendulum response.

The understanding of how and why Radionics works is adequately detailed in David Tansley's book Science and Magic, and the principles of thought transference apply to the pendulum usage. The following diagram can be explained as to how the link is made when questioning the universal source about your patient.

Consider a patient in another part of the world, far away from the practitioner. The patient's free will decides on approaching a practitioner for help (right brain thinking). His left brain prepares a sample or witness along with a written request for help and then mails this to the practitioner (left brain thinking). On receipt of the letter and sample the practitioner places it upon his instrument with certain cards as symbols (left brain thinking). The Practitioner then activates his pendulum and asks for degrees of deviation, or type of treatment required for this patient (right brain thinking). The circuit is then complete. The left and right brain of both patient and practitioner are satisfied that a logical and vital question is at hand. An instantaneous and correct answer will be given via the universal source, which was aware of the patient's ills long before the question was posed.

The pendulum will only give the correct answer to a problem if the patient has asked, or if you are aware of the universal needs of that patient.

The Universal Source or Godhead The Supreme Intelligence

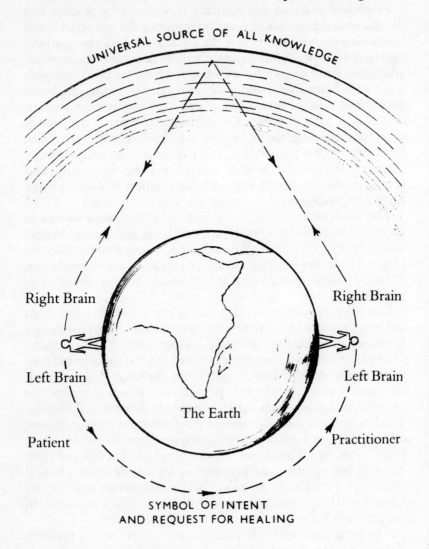

UNIVERSAL SOURCE OF ALL KNOWLEDGE

Right Brain

Right Brain

Left Brain

Left Brain

The Earth

Patient

Practitioner

SYMBOL OF INTENT
AND REQUEST FOR HEALING

You cannot ascertain information about a person if there is no intent, unless a relative, parent or friend acts in a surrogate way. Your pendulum will not give answers to material questions for material gain, when there is no universal need for the answer. You may get a reaction from your pendulum but it will be of your own left brain origin and of little use.

Dowsers searching for water hold in their left brain the need for water to be found, a universal need. The pendulum will react when the underground stream is crossed, the interface is between the Dowsers right brain and the universal source of vibration and not the pendulum reacting to a signal emanating from the ground.

We have seen how pendulum reaction can answer qualitative questions involving a simple yes or no, but the pendulum reaction can also indicate degrees or proportions, in other words, a quantative assessment. This can be obtained with absolute precision, so that records and charts can be maintained.

The essential conditions for the successful use of the pendulum are a quiet mind and clear specific questions. Without this, misleading answers will be obtained.

It is not that the pendulum will not respond, but that the indications will be unreliable if the question is ambiguous.

The pendulum, in fact, must not be used for trivialities, such as guessing which overturned playing card is a spade or heart, and trying to find which closed container has sugar or salt inside.

Pendulum training is a serious matter and teachers should be well versed in the universal concepts and the pendulum training instrument. It is essential to remember always that one is attempting to ask questions of an intelligent universe possessing a consciousness of superior order. Any attempt to communicate with the higher level must be undertaken with a proper sense of scale.

2. The principle employed is that by rotating the knob (A), the disc (B) may be made electrically positive, neutral, or negative relative to the screw-head (C), and the centre-zero meter (D) will indicate thus:

(i) For Positive

(ii) For Neutral

(iii) For Negative

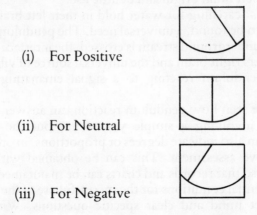

3. The conventional pendulum response, *with cord held between thumb and first finger* is:

(i) For Positive

(ii) For Neutral

(iii) For Negative

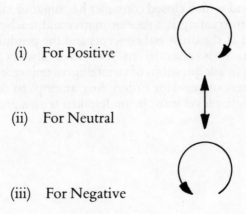

4.   It will be seen, therefore, that the meter needle indicates the correct behaviour of the pendulum.

5.   The method of training is simply to have the trainee deliberately make the pendulum behave in accordance with the meter's indication. After a certain amount of practice in this manner, the pendulum will be found to be 'ahead' of the deliberate movement – in other words, the trainee is starting to detect the polarity of the plate.

6.   In the early stages, the trainee should place a finger of the left hand on the screw head (C) as this increases his apparent sensitivity; but this should be discontinued as soon as possible.

7.   As skill and certainty are gained, a piece of card may be placed over the meter to obscure its indications and practice in detecting its reading, or setting to a given reading should be undertaken.

Notes: 1.   Care should be taken to switch off when not in use.

2.   To replace the battery, the top panel should be gently lifted off, after unscrewing the four corner screws.

3.   The battery used is a standard PP9 or equivalent. It *MUST* be 9 volts.

CHAPTER NINE

The Radionic Analysis

"It is important that twentieth century man adapts a path to wisdom and gives absolute priority to the study and harnessing of the purer energy which is still showered continuously on the earth by the Cosmic God."

Herbert Weaver
Divining the Primary Sense

The Radionic Analysis is a procedure using symbols and rituals to establish degrees of deviaion in subtle body energies, chakra centres and formative energy of the structures of the physical anatomy. The information obtained being the degrees of deviation from optimum function of the etheric energy or formative energy controlling the centre, gland or organ we are measuring. The resultant information is not the exact state or condition of the physical organ in pathological terms, Radionics is not a physical process. We are measuring the functional and structural integrity as every physical organ has its counterpart which is built from etheric, astral and mental matter.

Practitioners should familiarise themselves with the subtle anatomy analysis sheet on page 76. This sheet is a guide to the type of information required and can be changed to suit the individual concerned. It does however give a good basis on which to work when starting out in radionics.

The right hand side of the sheet is concerned with the subtle bodies, and chakra centres. Their degrees from optimum function, whether underactive or overactive and the factor which is causing this activity.

The degrees of intensity of other factors are also checked, for they may well be relevant when looking for causes' of disharmony in the subtle body.

The centre of the chart has the space for inserting the causal body in total, as well as the breakdown for further personal ray energy analysis. The personal energies, or low self, are mental, astral and physical etheric, and their totality being the whole of the personal body.

The left hand side of the chart has listed the pre-physical organ systems and structures, with degrees for mean and worst point readings.

This analysis sheet is used in conjunction with the Rae Analyser which is shown on page 77.

The analyser consists of the main instrument into which three slots are cut to accept the data cards, and has four switches and a pointer dial for potency selection.

The flat chart holder, incorporating the magnetised rubber sheet plugs into the main body of the instrument.

Two laminated, washable charts are supplied with the instrument, one for analysis, the other for remedy selection.

The analyser is extremely flexible in application, and users will undoubtedly develop their individual method of employing it. Nevertheless, the following is offered as one effective method.

IT MUST BE EMPHASISED THAT THE OPERATION OF THE ANALYSER IS DEPENDANT UPON THE SENSITIVITY OF THE USER, AND THEIR ABILITY TO OPERATE A PENDULUM.

In preparing to use the analyser, connect the chart holder to the instrument by inserting its two plugs in the sockets provided, without crossing the wires, and set all switches to OFF and the MEAN/MAX switch at MAX.

The potency selection dial is set at 'O', and the analysis chart palced on the chart holder.

Place the patient's witness (preferably a few hairs sealed between two sticky labels) in the circle labelled 'patient's witness' on the chart. Write the patient's name and date of birth on one side of the sticky label.

SUBTLE ANATOMY ANALYSIS ACCORDING TO MAGNETO GEOMETRIC APPLICATIONS.

NAME		ADDRESS		FEES
D.O.B		SYMPTOMS		DATE
				G.T.R.

DEGREE OF DEVIATION FROM FUNCTIONAL PERFECTION

STRUCTURE — DEGREE AT WORST POINT

0 10 20 30 40 50 60 70 80 90 100

STRUCTURE:

- AURAL
- VISUAL
- C.N.S.
- SYMP. NER
- PARA. SYMP. NER
- ENDOCRINE
- RESPIRATORY
- CARDIO - VASCULAR
- GASTRO INTESTINAL
- LIVER
- URINARY
- ADRENAL
- GENITAL
- BLOOD
- LYMPH
- SKELETAL
- MUSCULAR
- TISSUES
- CELLS
- SKIN
- FLUIDS
- TEETH
- TONSILS

CAUSAL RAY

- + -
- + -
- + -

PERSONAL RAY

- M
- A
- P/E

DEGREE OF DEVIATION FROM THE CAUSAL BODY ENERGIES AFFECTING OPTIMUM FUNCTION OF ___.

UNDERACTIVITY — OPTIMUM — OVERACTIVITY

100 90 80 70 60 50 40 30 20 10 0 10 20 30 40 50 60 70 80 90 100   FACTOR

- MENTAL
- ASTRAL
- ETHERIC
- NADIS — UN CO-ORD

- CROWN
- AJNA/BROW
- THROAT
- HEART
- SOLAR PLEXUS
- SACRAL
- BASE
- SPLEEN
- ALTA MAJOR

DEGREES OF OTHER FACTORS

0 10 20 30 40 50 60 70 80 90 100

- MIASMS TYPE
- DET. EFF. OF VACC.
- POISON
- TOXINS
- AUTOINTOXICATION

NOTES

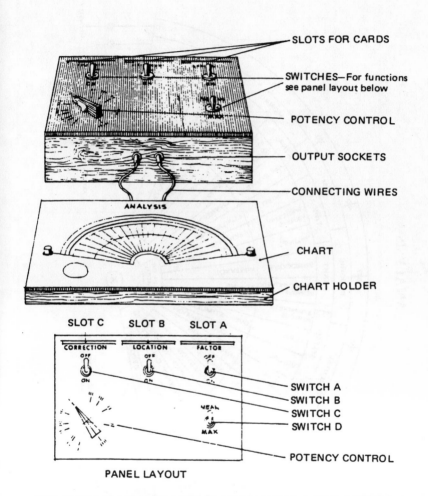

SLOTS FOR CARDS

SWITCHES—For functions see panel layout below

POTENCY CONTROL

OUTPUT SOCKETS

CONNECTING WIRES

ANALYSIS

CHART

CHART HOLDER

SLOT C   SLOT B   SLOT A

CORRECTION   LOCATION   FACTOR

OFF   OFF   OFF

ON   ON   ON

SWITCH A
SWITCH B
SWITCH C
SWITCH D

MEAN
MAX

POTENCY CONTROL

PANEL LAYOUT

IT MUST BE EMPHASISED THAT THE OPERATION
OF THIS INSTRUMENT IS DEPENDENT UPON THE
SENSITIVITY OF THE USER

ANALYSIS

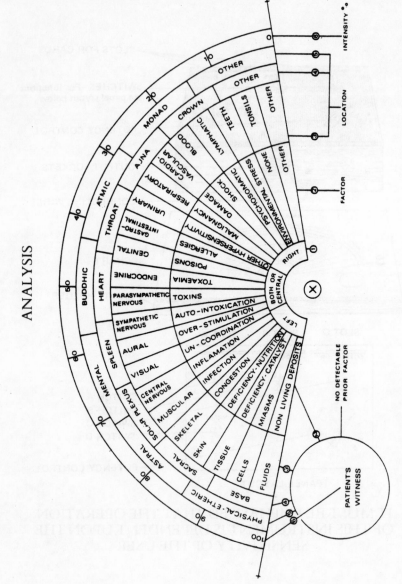

THE ANALYSIS PROCEDURE IS AS FOLLOWS

1.   Select the card labelled mental body and insert it, with name facing you, in the location slot and put the location switch at ON.

2.   Using scale 6 on the analyser chart, and your pendulum centred over 'X' and swinging along the 'O' line, pose the following question:

"WHAT IS THE DEGREE OF DEVIATION FROM FUNCTIONAL PERFECTION OF THE MENTAL BODY?"

The pendulum will measure off the degree of deviation. Make a mental note of the reading (example 60).

3.   With the pendulum still swinging at the measure degree of deviation (example 60) pose the second question.

"WHAT IS THE DEGREE OF DEVIATION FROM THE CAUSAL BODY ENERGIES AFFECTING THE OPTIMUM FUNCTIONING OF THE MENTAL BODY?"

The pendulum will do one of two things – stay at the measured degree or return to the 'O' line.

This information enables the practitioner to establish:

(a)   If the patient's causal body is responsible for the 60° deviation in the mental body (the pendulum has returned 'O') or

(b)   If the patient's 60° deviation is caused by the low self or environmental aspect (the pendulum stays at 60)

These procedures and reasoning have been more fully explained in chapter 7.

4.   With the pendulum centred over the 'X' and with your left finger pointing to scale 2, pose the following question:

"WHAT FACTOR IS CAUSING THE 60° DEVIATION IN THE MENTAL BODY?".

The pendulum will indicate which factor is involved i.e. Miasm.

5.   Select the factor card labelled ALL MIASMS and insert it, name facing you, in the FACTOR slot and put the factor switch to 'ON'.

6.   With the pendulum centred over the witness pose the following question:

"IS THE FACTOR CHOSEN (miasm) IN THE MENTAL BODY CAUSING A 60° UNDERACTIVITY?"

The pendulum will either give a positive or negative swing over the witness.

If the indication is yes to the question, place a dot at '60' opposite the mental level, left of optimum on the analysis sheet, and write the word MIASM in the factor column (showing where the miasm is causing 60° underactivity).

7. If the answer to question 3 was a swing back to 'O' then the interpretation is that the 60° deviation is coming from a higher level, i.e. a soul dictate. In this instance place a further dot on the optimum line, as it is optimum for the mental body to be affected by this miasm to a degree of 60°.

To interject briefly at this point, we have already established that the patient has an inherited miasm from either a previous lifetime or forefather and is causing an underactivity of the mental body. We know too that the miasms often reside in the base chakra area, and this example is at a mental level. We can see that the patient is perhaps suppressing the expression of the physical will-to-be. We know how the base chakra in the lower mental body links directly with the head chakras of the astral body. The practitioner can see a picture forming of the patient's condition after posing a few systematical questions of the mental body.

Now after noting on the analysis sheet 60° underactivity of the mental body and writing down the factor as a miasm, remove the cards and insert the next card labelled ASTRAL BODY in location slot, with location switch 'ON', all other switches must be 'OFF'.

Repeat the questions 2, 3, 4 and 5; i.e. measure the degree of deviation, check for any influence from the soul dictates that may reach down as far as the astral, check for the factor causing the disturbance, and if the disturbance is an underactivity or overactivity.

This sequence of questioning is repeated for Mental body, Astral body, Physical Etheric body and the Nadis.

THE CHAKRA CENTRES

The next area for investigation is the chakra centres, using the same procedures from crown to alta-major. Pose the question:

"WHAT IS THE DEGREE OF DEVIATION FROM FUN-CTIONAL PERFECTION OF THE CROWN CHAKRA?" and make a mental note.

If however there has been a subjective ray influence detrimentally affecting the subtle body areas, then the second question regarding how the causal ray influences affects the centres will be posed. If, however, there is no causal ray influence affecting the subtle bodies detrimentally then it is unnecessary to pose the second question for the centres.

Causal ray influence is indicated on the chart by a dot at 60° deviation and a dot at optimum.

If there is no causal influence then place a ring around the dot at 60° showing that the deviation is from the low self, the patient's environment or relationships with other people.

DEGREES OF INTENSITY FOR OTHER FACTORS is the next area for investigation and the procedure is as follows.

1.   Select the card labelled Miasms and insert in the factor slot with switch 'ON' and all others at 'OFF'.

2.   Centre the pendulum over 'X' and using scale 6, pose the question:

"WHAT IS THE DEGREE OF MIASMS AFFECTING THE SUBTLE BODIES OF THIS PATIENT?"

Note down the reading by placing a dot at the respective degree. This procedure is repeated for the factors of Miasms, Detrimental effects of vaccinations, poisons, toxins and autointoxication.

RAY ASPECTS

Next in the analysis procedure is the dowsing of the causal and personal Rays on which the patient is functioning. The procedure is briefly explained here, but will be more fully explained in Chapter 12, which will give details on how to interpret the influences of rays on the centres and in the relationships with certain progressive remedies.

To ascertain the causal ray, the practitioner must have a full knowledge and understanding of the rays, which areas of the subtle anatomy they influence, relationships between one ray and another, and from which areas in the causal body the rays emanate. The rays are identified by number when dowsing and the pendulum may be held over the patient's witness with no cards in the instrument and all switches at 'OFF'. Pose the question:

"IS THE PATIENT'S CAUSAL RAY 1" (watch for pendulum reaction) if none, then ask 2, 3, 4 and so forth until the pendulum gives a positive swing when the correct ray number is reached.

The same procedure applies when dowsing the rays of the low self; that is, the Mental ray, Astral ray and Physical Etheric ray. Lastly the ray of the Personality which governs all aspects of the low self and subtle bodies.

THE PHYSICAL STRUCTURES

The following procedure is used for examining the condition of the physical structures.

1. Place the card labelled Aural in the slot marked 'LOCATION', switch 'ON'; all other switches 'OFF'. The 'MEAN/MAX' switch at 'MEAN', and with the pendulum swinging along the 0° line and using scale 6 on the chart pose the question:

"WHAT IS THE DEGREE OF DEVIATION FROM FUNCTIONAL PERFECTION OF THE AURAL SYSTEM?" and note the reading.

2. Whilst the pendulum is still swinging over the registered degrees, place your left hand on the 'MEAN/MAX' switch and put it on to 'MAX', whilst at the same time posing the question:

"WHAT IS THE DEGREE AT WORST POINT?"

The pendulum will either stay swinging where it is, or it will move further round the scale and measure off the degree at worst point. Note the reading with a circle on the subtle anatomy analysis sheet.

Repeat this procedure for all the physical structures from Aural to Tonsils, placing the respective cards in sequence one at a time and noting the degrees of deviation and worst point measurements.

The subtle anatomy analysis sheet will look similar to the completed example on page 87.

Study this example whilst familiarising yourself with the procedures so far explained.

SELECTION OF OPTIMUM TREATMENTS

On completion of the analysis and study of the subtle anatomy analysis sheet the causative factors of the patient's ills will soon be recognisable. Our aim in Radionics is to establish the basic causes at a subtle level and to instigate treatments allowing the vital essence to flow freely again with the patient.

1.   REMEDY SELECTION.

With cards in the slots marked FACTOR and LOCATION (example) LOCATION – MENTAL BODY. FACTOR – ALL MIASMS and switches 'A' and 'B' at 'ON' ('MEAN/MAX' at 'MAX').

2.   Remove the analysis chart board from the chart holder and replace with the treatment chartboard.

3.   Place the patient's witness in the circle marked 'Patient's Witness'.

4.   Centre the pendulum over the patient's witness and pose the question:

"WHAT TYPE OF TREATMENT WILL IRRADICATE THE MIASMS FROM THE MENTAL BODY?"

5.   The pendulum will indicate which type of treatment on scale 6 (example could be colour).

6.   With your pendulum still over the patient's witness pose the question:

"WHAT IS THE INITIAL LETTER OF THE COLOUR" (i.e. perhaps Y meaning Yellow).

7.   Place the selected card Yellow in the correction slot C and turn the potency selection to 10MM.

8.   Remeasure the degree of deviation of the primary disorder against scale 7, and when the pendulum has settled at the measured degree, set switch to 'C' to 'ON'.

9.   The correct remedy (exact similimum) will result in the pendulum swinging back to 'O' unless there is a nutritional deficiency which cannot be remedied except by the administration of a substance.

10. Assuming the pendulum has settled over 'O' the potency control should be turned slowly anticlockwise until the pendulum begins to move away from 'O'. The correct potency of the selected remedy will then be indicated by the setting to

which the potency control has been reduced.

11. With pendulum centred over the patient's witness, pose the question:

"WHAT IS THE METHOD OF ADMINISTRATION?" and note the pendulum reaction.

12. With the pendulum centred over the patient's witness pose the question:

"WHAT IS THE FORECAST INTERVAL BETWEEN DOSES?" and note the reaction.

13. Lastly with the pendulum over the patient's witness pose the question:

"FOR HOW MANY DOSES?"

All the above information should be noted down on the patient's case history sheet, and the procedures 1 to 13 may be repeated for remedy selection for worst degree of the chakra centres and physical structures if indicated. Often one type of remedy indicated at a subtle body level will be suitable for the centres and physical body.

The book Dimensions of Radionics details a second and much quicker method for experienced practitioners that are interested only in the worst symptoms of disorder, without going through the procedure of a full subtle anatomy analysis as has been explained here. It should be emphasised however that before a practitioner uses the second method he should be fully versed in subtle anatomy principles. The subtle anatomy analysis sheet gives a complete picture of the patient's condition and relationships can be seen between subtle body influences, chakra centres and the glands these centres control. The analyser allows the practitioner to select the optimum treatment based on the causative factors.

Completed case history shown on page 87.

TREATMENT   PROCEDURES   AFTER   THE
COMPLETION OF THE ANALYSIS

Primary treatment should be based upon the highest degree of deviation or the highest dimension of disturbance in the Mental, Astral and Physical Etheric bodies.

Secondary treatments should be based upon the chakra, ray relationship and the physical symptoms related to that chakra centre, or the energetic relationship of chakra centres.

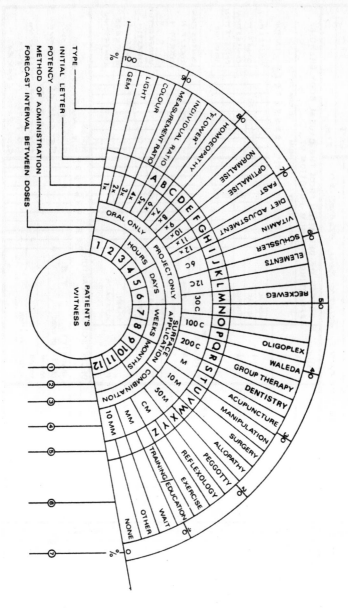

TREATMENT

NAME	MRS. J. SMITH	ADDRESS	SUSSEX, U.K.	FEES
				DATE
D.O.B	3.11.1947	SYMPTOMS	MIGRAINE, SCIATIC PAIN, BLADDER DIS.	G.T.R.

DEGREE OF DEVIATION FROM FUNCTIONAL PERFECTION

DEGREE AT WORST POINT — scale 0 10 20 30 40 50 60 70 80 90 100

STRUCTURE	Note
AURAL	
VISUAL	
C.N.S.	SCIATIC NERVE
SYMP. NER	
PARA. SYMP. NER	
ENDOCRINE	PIT. + ADREN.
RESPIRATORY	
CARDIO-VASCULAR	CONSTIPATION
GASTRO INTESTINAL	
LIVER	INFLAM.
URINARY	OVERSTIM.
ADRENAL	
GENITAL	
BLOOD	
LYMPH	SUBLUX.
SKELETAL	
MUSCULAR	
TISSUES	
CELLS	
SKIN	
FLUIDS	
TEETH	
TONSILS	

DEGREE OF DEVIATION FROM THE CAUSAL BODY ENERGIES AFFECTING OPTIMUM FUNCTION OF ___

UNDERACTIVITY — OPTIMUM — OVERACTIVITY
scale 100 90 80 70 60 50 40 30 20 10 0 10 20 30 40 50 60 70 80 90 100

CAUSAL RAY: - + - , - + - , - + -

	FACTOR
MENTAL	CONGESTION
ASTRAL	OVERSTIM.
ETHERIC	CONGESTION
NADIS	CONGESTION / UN CO-ORD

PERSONAL RAY: M, A, P/E

	FACTOR
CROWN	CONGESTION
AJNA/BROW	OVERSTIM.
THROAT	OVERSTIM.
HEART	" " "
SOLAR PLEXUS	UNDERACTIVE
SACRAL	OVERSTIM.
BASE	OVERSTIM.
SPLEEN	BLOCKAGE
ALTA MAJOR	CONGESTION

DEGREES OF OTHER FACTORS

MIASMS TYPE	T.B.
DET. EFF. OF VACC.	
POISON	
TOXINS	
AUTOINTOXICATION	

NOTES

T.B. MIASM IS BEING
BLOCKED IN ITS FLOW
BECAUSE OF EMOTIONAL
OVERACTIVITY.
TREAT WITH YELLOW TO
T.B MIASM IN MENTAL
BODY BASE CHAKRA.

Other treatments are based on the patient's symptomology and the prescribing of oral remedies. This acts to continue the patient's intent for healing.

Treatment procedures should all be based upon the re-balancing of the chakra centres and the compatibility of the rays, whether as a dictate of that patient's central identity or the environment.

TREATMENTS FOR MRS JANE SMITH – AS PER SUBTLE ANATOMY ANALYSIS

1.   Yellow, Potency 1M to the T.B. Miasm Mental Body Base Chakra – 1 dose only.

2.   Emerald Green, Potency 1M to Astral Body Head Chakra – 1 projection only.

3.   Dr Bach combination of Rock Water/Olive/Impatiens orally – 4 times a day for 1 week.

4.   Homoeopathic Ignatia 6× for 3 days – 2 day break followed by Homoeopathic Gelsemium 6c for 1 week.

This patient reported no further migraines or sciatica after approximately three weeks. There was a slight re-occurrence at the sixth week but this subsided with further Bach Remedies and projections to the astral body head chakras. A year later the patient was still in good health.

CHAPTER TEN

Radionic Treatment at a Distance

"The universal mind is so clearly linked to the very process and nature of Radionic diagnosis and treatment."

David Tansley
Dimensions of Radionics

It is important here to recall what has been written in the last few chapters and remind the reader that a proper perspective between the use of the practitioner's mind and the instruments is needed when dealing with Radionic treatment.

The instruments now explained together with the procedures used, are necessary for the left brain logic of the practitioner, the actual healing is done by the right brain link up with practitioner and patient.

The treatment instruments when used Radionically are all part of symbols and rituals – procedures necessary in distant healing.

THE TRIPLET INSTRUMENT

The most popular of the Rae treatment instruments shown on page 92 was developed from the success of the twin remedy location instrument.

The triplet has the advantage of the third slot. This enables the practitioner to use the cards immediately from the analyser when he has found the correction for the worst location and factor.

OPERATION

1. The correction card is placed in slot A and the potency control set to the potency obtained during the analysis.

2.   The factor card is placed in slot B and the potency control set at 'O'.

3.   The location card is placed in slot C and the potency control set at 'O'.

4.   Place the patient's witness in the circular plastic phial provided and place in the well of the instrument.

5.   Put switches D & E at 'ON'.

6.   With pendulum centred over the well and swinging in a straight line, and your left hand on the potency control of the factor slot B, turn the potency control clockwise until a positive clockwise rotation is registered by the pendulum. This is the necessary potency of the factor card for the patient.

7.   Repeat the procedure 6 for the location card in slot C.

8.   Plug into socket 'F' of the triplet instrument the jack plug from the interrupter.

9.   With the pendulum centred and swinging over the well of the triplet, place your left hand on the control knob of the interrupter and slowly tune from SEDATE towards STIMULATE.

10.   When a positive or clockwise giration of the pendulum is noted this is the right frequency of pulsations needed from the interrupter for optimum treatment.

The interrupter now has the facility to sedate and stimulate treatments. Diagram shows an interrupter connected from the mains to the triplet instrument.

The period of time required for projections differs for each patients, ten seconds to two minutes are average times, longer periods of treatment may be administered for ACUTE ailments.

Remedies for oral use may be made in this instrument by using a remedy card in slot C only. No combination remedies can be made in this instrument as it is wired differently to a standard M.G.A. homoeopathic simulator.

When using the instrument for potentising sac lac or water switches D & E must be "OFF".

When using sac lac as the medium six minutes is the requisite time for potentisation; if water is the medium, one minute.

Selection of potency is controlled by potency control C.

Switch D controls slot A and switch E controls slot B.

The use of this triplet instrument allows the practitioner to project his healing influences to his patient on the thought waves from his right brain function. The instrument provides the total back up for left brain logic by having the symbols of correction and location to be treated at their correct potency or proportion. The practitioner is restoring the vital essence to his patient and re-establishing the boundaries of energies with correct potency.

INTERRUPTER

An electronic interrupter housed in an alloy box, operating from AC mains – either 240 volts 50 cycles or 110 volts 60 cycles, provides the necessary pulsations to convert any of the Rae instruments into projectors from which the remedy may be administered via a sample of the patient's hair.

INTERRUPTER DISTRIBUTION BOX

A single interrupter will operate several instruments simultaneously, and a small junction box, and four additional leads, each with a jack at either end is all that is needed to enable it to do this.

The diagram on page 93 shows how 3 cards can be used in the triplet, i.e.:

Normalise	Base Chakra	Kidneys
	or	
Blue	Throat Chakra	Respiratory
	or	
Pearl	Ajna Chakra	Visual
	and	
Stannum Iodatum	T.B. Miasm	Mental Body Base

Now this leads to a very interesting aspect of Radionic treatment, for it is possible to treat a particular chakra centre in a Mental or Astral body area. You will recall that in previous chapters I have referred to the diagram on page 17. Most Radionic Practitioners have seen the diagram, and it should be studied in great detail.

The flow of energy from centre to centre is important and, the relationship from one chakra to another, and which rays should predominate naturally through each related centre.

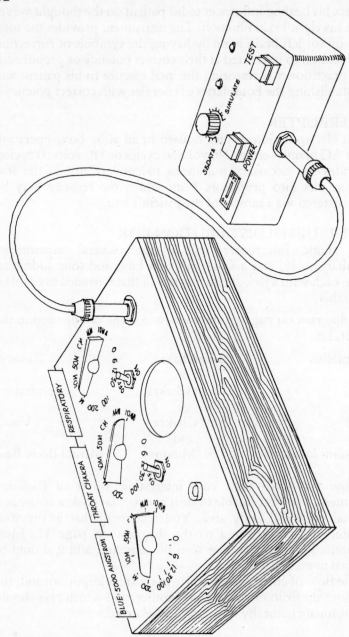

Triplet – Standard Instrument and Interrupter

93

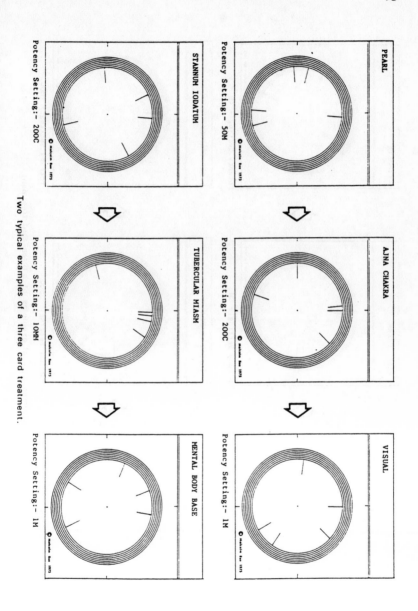

Two typical examples of a three card treatment.

94

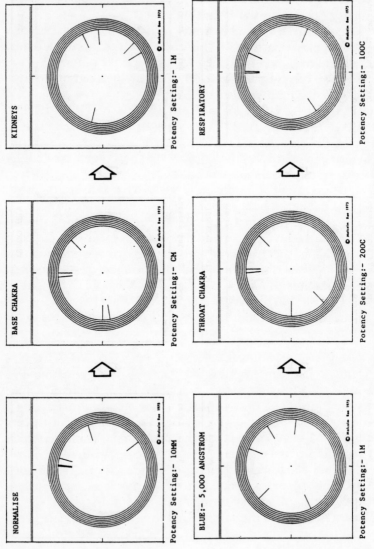

Two further typical examples of a three card treatment.

In the chapter on miasms, I said 'let the energy flow' and this is what we can achieve with the use of the triplet instrument. We direct energy from centre to centre, and for this purpose I had simulator cards prepared as in Appendix B.

These are the K.M. subtle body cards having a location of a centre in a particular body. This gives a greater accuracy when treating or setting in motion energy through the centres.

Hence we can couple up two triplets as in the diagram on page 94 and give the following treatments.

COLOUR – MENTAL BODY BASE – ASTRAL BODY HEAD – ASTRAL BODY BASE – PHYSICAL ETHERIC HEAD – PHYSICAL ETHERIC BASE.

Treatments such as these clear the blockages created by miasms, trauma and shock and allow a free flow of energy from the soul and causal body dictates, this is what true healing is, to allow the patient to be an expression of their soul dictate.

I had a further treatment card designed, not only for a specific need, but to be given as an initial projection to all new patients, thus allowing the patient to display to the practitioner the relevant degrees of deviation, and thus bring to the forefront of the practitioners mind the basic causative factors. This card is labelled "ALIGNMENT OF CHAKRAS WITH SOUL".

The full interpretation being (restore all major chakras to the awakened state as directed by the patient's own soul ray).

THE 4 SECTION STANDARD K.M. INSTRUMENT

A further instrument now available to homoeopathic and radionic practitioners is the 4 section K.M. standard. This instrument grew out of my using the 4 section multiple remedy simulator. I had the switching changed and wiring adjustments made and M.G.A. have made this instrument available which can produce up to 4 different remedies in combination as before, but has the added feature of giving a 4 section radionic treatment.

This allows an extra card to be used to complete a basic healing instruction radionically speaking.

We are all aware of the subtle body controlling chakras and the glands governed, therefore the 4 section instrument allows us to treat as follows:

REMEDY – SUBTLE BODY – CHAKRA CENTRE – ORGAN/GLAND.

96

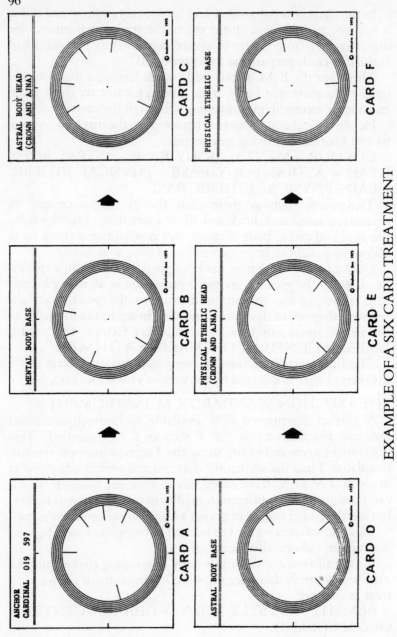

EXAMPLE OF A SIX CARD TREATMENT

CARD A

ANCHOR
CARDINAL 019 597

CARD B

MENTAL BODY BASE

CARD C

ASTRAL BODY HEAD
(CROWN AND AJNA)

CARD D

ASTRAL BODY BASE

CARD E

PHYSICAL ETHERIC HEAD
(CROWN AND AJNA)

CARD F

PHYSICAL ETHERIC BASE

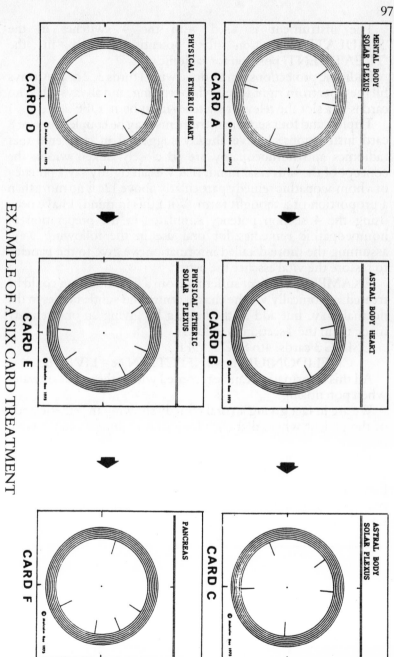

EXAMPLE OF A SIX CARD TREATMENT

The instrument is used with the 4 switches in the 'SIMULATE' position for potentising, and in the 'TREATMENT' position for radionic use.

Radionic projections can be done with 4 cards 3, 2 or 1. Always fill the slots from right to left when treating, and always when no card is in a slot the relevant switches must be at 'OFF'.

Triplets and four section instruments may be coupled for 6 or 8 card instructions. I have already suggested in chapter 6 that radionics and homoeopathy are so closely linked within the concept of the universal mind, that we can rightly say a potency of a homoeopathic remedy particularly above 12c is no more than a proportion of a thought form. With this in mind, I have been using the 4 section potency simulator in the preparation of homoeopathic remedies for oral use in the following way, assuming the more detailed information we give to the patients to restore the vital essence the better.

EXAMPLE: a patient suffering from a liver infection could be treated radionically via the chakra centre and subtle bodies in the normal way, but add to the healing by giving an oral remedy made up in the 4 section as follows:

USING 3 cards. 4th SLOT 'OFF'.

CHELIDONIUM 6c – INFECTION 6c – LIVER 6c

All this information can be recorded within the sac lac or water when potentising.

We are in fact giving an oral remedy showing the etheric body of the patient where that chelidonium is required, and for what purpose.

When the practitioner tunes his mind to this way of administering coded instruction to his patients on a regular daily basis, and the patient participates with the symbols of taking his pills daily, the healing process is dramatic and is greatly speeded up.

Standard 4 Section K.M. Type

CHAPTER ELEVEN

The Intolerance Syndrome: Homoeopathic Simulation

"Radionic therapy seeks to use only natural forces to combat disease and this attempt to understand and co-operate with nature characterises the development of this therapy."
Lavender Dower & Liz. Baerlein
Healing with Radionics

How many patients do we see that have transgressed the laws of nature by gluttony, lack of sleep, smoking and by the abuse of alcohol.

Fortunately, nature is tolerant and will allow us to help these patients, but only if we as practitioners can guide the patient along the path of life in a more harmonious way with the universe. The patients themselves, having the will to attain this attitude is important. In radionics we can be educators as well as healers.

It has been proven homoeopathically that 'like cures like', and so the clamour of today's patients suffering from food intolerances or allergies can be helped. Most allergy problems do have a deep seated origin, recognisable by radionics when dowsing in the Astral body in particular. Very often the emotional trauma or outburst will trigger off the allergic reaction.

Allergies today are mainly intolerance of food additives rather than the patient being classified as an allergic individual. It is these additives and toxins in food that the body has difficulty in coping with.

THE RAE MAGNETIC
HOMOEOPATHIC POTENCY PREPARER

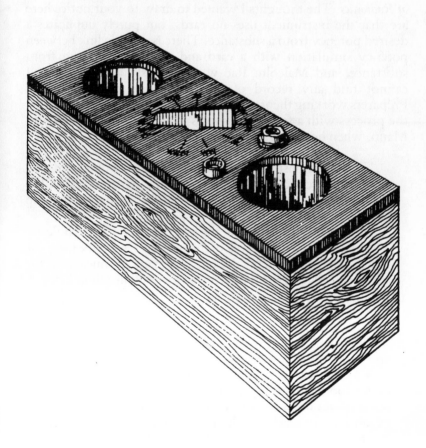

Rudolf Steiner in Spiritual Science and Medicine tells us that to give a man small amounts of that which seems intolerable to him only strengthens his constitution, so we we can treat like with like in a homoeopathic way.

The most suitable instrument for the problem of allergies is the Homoeopathic Potency Preparer, illustrated on page 101.

The instructions for use are competently described in *Dimensions of Radionics*. The thoughts I wanted to draw to your notice here are that the instrument uses no cards, but purely duplicates a desired potency from a substance. There is a subtle link between potency simulation with a card and potency preparing from substance, and Malcolm Rae was obviously aware of this. I cannot find any record of his explanation of the Potency Preparers working theory, but I can relate to you my thoughts on the process with a few more quotes from the *Round Art* by Tad Mann, when he tells of the POINT and CIRCLE:

"The relationship between the centre point and the circumference indicates the nature of the centre as a FOCUS and of the periphery as DISPERSION, bridging the gap between the ideal and the real.

The centre is the scintella, the breath of life of the whole.

It corresponds to the yolk of the egg, the seed in the fruit, the sun in the solar system, the heart in man, the nucleus in the atom, and all these are the germ and focus of the whole being."

and

"The centre point is, as it were, the origin of the spherical body, the outer surface, the image of the innermost point as well as the way to arrive at it, and the outer surface can be understood as coming about by an infinite expansion of the point itself until a certain equality of all the individual acts of expansion are reached. The point spreads itself out over the extension so that point and surface are identical except for the fact that the ratio of density and extension is reversed. Hence there is exists everywhere between point and surface the most beautiful harmony, connection, relation, proportion and commersurability. And although centre, surface and distance are manifestly three, yet they are One, so that not one of them could even be imagined to be absent without destroying the whole."

To add in my own thoughts here, that is the card symbol information or pattern, used in the instruments is taken off, so to speak, at the centre point by a wire surrounded by the circular magnet. This wire travels to the potency control or potential divider and then to the circular well of the instrument.

Therefore the information transmitted from the card to the well is contained in the cards centre point.

The centre point is the energy, the periphery, the boundary of that energy. In the Potency Preparer using no cards the wire is taken from the magnetised circular input well, through the potency control to the centre point of the output well again circular.

BOTH SYSTEMS USING THE POINT WITHIN THE CIRCLE PRINCIPLE.

The Rae card is the symbol of the universal thought pattern for a remedy and this information is contained in the relationship between the radii which is obviously replicated in the centre point of the card. Therefore the quotations from the "Round Art of Astrology" which are statements from Jung & Kepler are being used today in our radionic and homoeopathic therapies. All information contained in a circle whether it is a drawn pattern or substance is also replicated in the centre of the circle and can be transmitted down a wire, the magnetism being the carrier wave.

Those of you who have read Malcolm Rae's paper 'Homoeopathy up to date', will be familiar with the following diagrams.

I trust you will now see the importance of the centre point within the circle when considering homoeopathic simulation instruments and the representation of the whole being contained in the centre.

Man can also be symbolised by the circle with a centre point, as man is always at the centre of the circle wherever he stands on earth.

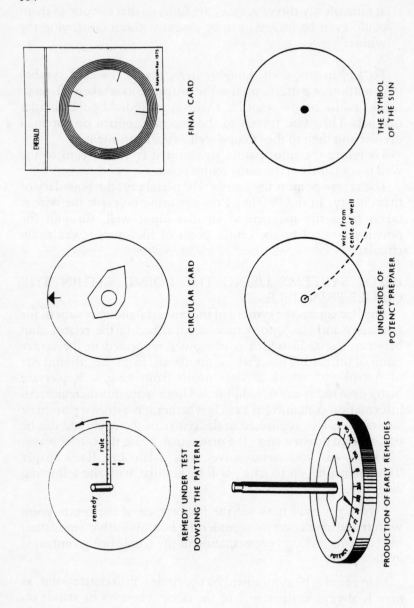

FINAL CARD

EMERALD

© Malcolm Rae 1975

THE SYMBOL
OF THE SUN

CIRCULAR CARD

UNDERSIDE OF
POTENCY PREPARER

wire from
centre of well

REMEDY UNDER TEST
DOWSING THE PATTERN

rule

remedy

PRODUCTION OF EARLY REMEDIES

POTENCY

Returning to the allergy question, I find secondary causes within patients to be social rather than medical.

With high powered marketing and advertising methods today, we are compelled or advised to eat extra kinds of foods or specialist foods, as well as other items or luxuries from the external world. This makes us more unsociable. We become selfish and greedy for that which is mine. We create these barriers to the natural flow of energy, that interfere with the natural law of universal boundaries.

There is great value in families eating together at the table, the mere possibility of being with others as we eat and drink has great social value.

There is an importance to be placed upon visualisation of what we eat. Give a thought to nature's process of life giving to the plant. When we eat, those life giving forces activate our innate thinking processes. Remember that every digestive organ in the body has a two fold function, one in the organic sphere, the other spiritual. Do not forget to nourish them both.

Rudolph Steiner tells us in Spiritual Science and Medicine:

"If man be left alone in individual isolation, not only as regards conscious processes but also in all organic activities, he develops all manner of appetites and anti-appetites".

To gratify appetites beyond a certain limit, does not strengthen our organs, but hypertrophies them and brings about degeneration. To go too far in yielding to the antipathies of the organism, causes profound damage to the whole organisation. Whilst on the other hand, gradually accustoming a man to that which seems unsuitable to him always strengthens his constitution.

Steiner tells us again.

"Moreover smaller dosages of substances used pharmaceutically have the same relation to highly potentised dosages as sympathy is to antipathy, in the human organism. High potency can have the opposite effect from low potency."

Therefore give a high potency of the allergen for the intolerance syndrome. This fact has been recognised in the use of the Dr Bach Flower remedies. A remedy can be used both positively and negatively for different individuals. It is then important, when dealing with allergies, to radionically establish the substance causing the allergic reaction. Introduce the substance to the patient either by using infinitesimal doses or homoeopathic dosage. This homoeopathic dosage can be prepared in the Potency Preparer using the allergen in the input well, and preparing a potency in sac lac form.

The advantage of the homoeopathic dosage lies in the fact that some poisonous or toxic substances within the food may be causing the intolerance, and by administration of the potency there will be traces of the poison or toxin in that Homoeopathic potency that will activate the vital essence within the patient, to be more tolerant of the food.

SOME SPECIAL APPLICATIONS OF THE POTENCY PREPARER ARE AS FOLLOWS

1. Nosodes from patient's blood, urine, sputum etc.
2. Remedies from hair of a particular animal to which the patient is allergic.
3. Remedies prepared from flowers, foodstuffs even tobacco for those who find smoking intolerable.
4. Remedies from gems or chemicals and poisons or substances where the representation of the therapeutic characteristic required extends beyond the chemical composition.

In preparing remedies for allergies I have given a few examples of materials from which I have made homoeopathic potencies: CHEESE, MILK, BUTTER, WHEAT, DETERGENT, HOUSE DUST, CATS HAIR, HORSE AND DOGS HAIR, TOBACCO, ASPIRIN, ANTIBIOTICS, CIGARS, LEMONS, FEATHERS, SOAP and many others. Always remember that it is very often a deep seated, hereditary or emotional trauma that can spark off an allergic reaction. As well as administering the potency of the allergen, you must treat the cause in the subtle body that sparked off the reaction.

CHAPTER TWELVE

Flowers and Rays: Progressive Remedies

"The lords of the seven rays which pour forth from the spiritual sun are sometimes known as the sons of flame, or the angels from the throne of God. From these seven rays all creation comes into being. All mineral, plant, animal and human life is permeated by these planetary forces."

Joan Hodgson
Planetary Harmonies

The spirit of man chooses the exact time of his incarnation into physical matter, which is governed by universal laws and planetary positions.

In Radionic Analysis we can establish the rays on which a person is functioning, and with the birth sign and rising sign if possible, can ascertain that person's virtues, vices, glamours and the path of life they should be following.

Radionics is now progressing towards an educational and progressive therapy by helping patients find the path, by radionically projecting to them, or supplying remedies that will awaken within them the ray attribute and expression for which they incarnated.

The rays and their attributes can be studied in detail from Alice Bailey's 'Esoteric Psychology' books 1 and 2 – and Appendix G at the back of this book.

After a few years of using the rays in my radionic work, I find an increasing link with certain Dr Bach flower remedies, gems, colours, and the patient's birth date.

On studying and researching some basic astrology and further work on Dr Bach, I found a complete relationship between all these factors and remedies. So much so that I put together a basic chart of the rays and remedies and found that the seven relationship to the twelve was confirmed by many writers. It also appeared that remedies do have a two fold therapeutic effect: that is a remedy can be suitable for positive attributes of a patient, and can help the negative in another, relative to the rays on which they are functioning.

We know from years of experience, and have had confirmed by the Dr Bach Centre, all the positive and negative aspects of the flower remedies. They all relate to the seven rays. Dr Bach in his wisdom divided the flower remedies into seven sections and these seven sections can be related to the rays, virtues and vices. As we know, Dr Bach was devoted to the discovery of the 'Twelve Healers' and later the fully thirty-eight remedies, which he divided into seven. Flowers of the field that would treat the emotional nature of man rather than his physical symptoms.

As far as we know, he was not concerned with astrology, but his obvious, close observation of human nature and sickness during his orthodox medical practice led him to the conclusion that all physical symptoms had their roots in the disharmonies between the causal and personality. In terms of our study of the rays, we would call it incompatible ray influence between the soul and the low self. The low self having free will does, sometimes, choose wrong rays emanating from the convictions of other human beings and the general environment stress to which we are subjected, as well as the tests we have to take during our stay at this university of the earth, which subject us to rays from the throng of past personalities.

One example is the recommendation by Dr Bach of Red Chestnut for those who are anxious about the welfare of others. This comes under the rulership of Jupiter which is the colour blue, and is ray 2, functioning through the heart chakra. Willow is for those having resentment for their misfortunes, governed by the moon, colour orange, ray 4, and functioning through the brow chakra.

We know the chakra centres control the endocrine glands, therefore patients with apparent symptoms, due to glandular malfunction, for example left eye, ears or nervous system from a pituitary gland imbalance can be treated by willow, as it is a remedy born out of the universal mind on ray 4. It will heal the person with symptoms related to ray 4, brow chakra.

The use of remedies for progressive purposes is all important in healing today. We must allow the patient to express their soul dictates via the causal ray, the ray carries all the formative information for the physical from the source within the universe. It is the work of the remedy to keep the ray balanced and allow the stream of universal knowledge to flow. Homoeopathic and radionic treatments function at pre-material levels.

A further quote from Dr Bach and 'Heal Thyself'.

"Separation is impossible, for as soon as a beam of light is cut off from its source, it ceases to exist.

"Thus we may comprehend a little of the impossibility of separateness, as although each ray may have its individuality, it is nevertheless part of the great central creative power."

Alice Bailey tells us,

"That seven great rays exist in the cosmos, and one of these rays is subdivided to constitute the 'seven rays' which wielded by our Solar Logos, form the basis of endless variations in the creators system of worlds."

These seven rays may be described as the seven channels which all beings have within the solar system. The seven characteristics or modifications of life, for it is not to humanity only that these rays apply, but to the seven kingdoms as well.

Planetary influence and the rays system and relationship with man has up to now been little understood, but every planet is a focal point through which forces and energies circulate and flow ceaselessly, and these energies emanate from the universe itself, of which our own planet earth is a part and the sun is our centre.

Man's health and direction of life is influenced totally by this universal system, and in radionics we can establish and check the related planets, houses and their effects.

Every human being is found to be functioning on one or more of the seven rays.

Alice Bailey tells us that each one of the rays is the recipient and custodian of energies from:
1.   The Seven Solar Systems.
2.   The Twelve Constellations.

THE RAYS

The causal body energies comprise of the central identity ray, along with the positive and negative attributes from the rays of the past personalities; the predominant ray becomes the central identity.

The causal ray number we dowse during the radionic analysis is this central identity, but practitioners will realise that major influences from the previous personalities of the past filter down to the personal self during this lifetime, travelling on this central identity ray; this is, of course, the natural evolutionary process of man.

These supplementary influences and ray numbers can be dowsed and clues are given to us in the form of time and date of birth, race and country of origin chosen by the incoming soul at incarnation, as well as the chosen name, which gives resonance to the vibration of the personal self; these are the clues related to the rays of the past.

The causal body energies endeavour to bring the Mental, Astral and Physical Etheric bodies into line, and develop a personal ray that is compatible with causal body dictates.

During a person's lifetime, Mental, Astral and Physical Etheric bodies move towards and away from the central causal identity, because of personality traits travelling on that central identity, as well as the personal ray of the low self being influenced by the environment and convictions of others; this alone causes the dynamics of personality.

Health, harmony and progression will only occur when the personal ray mirrors or balances the energies of the causal self. Note that the dynamic energy exchange between chakra centres here is very important. When this occurs and the personal ray is the mask of the causal identity ray, then the purpose has been achieved and the progression is made for the totality of the causal body expression in this lifetime.

The Seven Rays are as follows:

THE RAYS OF ASPECT
1st ray – The ray of power, will and purpose.
2nd ray – The ray of love and wisdom.
3rd ray – The ray of active creative intelligence.

THE RAYS OF ATTRIBUTE
4th ray – The ray of harmony through conflict.
5th ray – The ray of concrete science or knowledge.
6th ray – The ray of idealism or devotion.
7th ray – The ray of order or ceremonial magic.

Every human is basically an expression of two ray forces.
The ray of the soul (subjective energy) causal.
The ray of the personality (objective energy).
The subjective can be broken down into seven rays, and the objective into three rays.

Every form in nature and every human being, is found upon one or other of the seven rays. A ray confers, through its energy, physical conditions, and determines the quality of the emotional nature, it colours the mental body, and it controls the distribution of energy, for the rays are different kinds of vibration, and govern a particular chakra in the body through which distribution is made. Each ray predisposes a man to certain strengths and weaknesses, and constitutes his principle of limitation, as well as endowing him with capacity. It governs the method of his relations to other human types and is responsible for his reactions in form to other life forms. It gives him his colouring and quality, his general tone on the three planes of the personality, and it moulds his physical appearance.

1st ray	Red	Crown chakra
2nd ray	Blue	Heart chakra
3rd ray	Yellow	Throat chakra
4th ray	Orange	Brow chakra

5th ray	Green	Sacral chakra
6th ray	Violet	Solar Plexus chakra
7th ray	Indigo	Base chakra

Following is a chart of relationships of suggested remedies to be used as a guide with rays.

NOTES ON JEFFERY FROM SOUTH AFRICA

1.   The patient with very little physical symptoms is a classic for treating via the rays.

2.   There is no deviation from causal body influences. Rays 5 and 7 go well together.

3.   7th ray base chakra at a Soul level causing slight over-stimulation in base chakra is normal.

4.   If a practitioner tried Radionically to put the chakra back to 'O' it would soon revert to +50.

5.   The problem here lies in the Mental ray and the Astral ray (4th), being incompatible with the 5th and 7th rays.

6.   4th ray 'harmony through conflict' on Mental/Astral level is because of a reactive relationship. This is causing overstimulation in the Mental Body and hypersensitivity in the Astral Body and inflammation in the Physical/Etheric and Nadis.

7.   Energy unco-ordination from Physical/Etheric – Nadis – to the nervous system via the 4th ray influence. 4th ray works via the brow and controls the nervous system.

TREATMENTS

 (i) Radionics

A projection of the colour Orange at a potency of 1M to the brow chakra.

(ii) Homoeopathy

The Flower remedy 'Crab Apple' as 4th ray remedy for despondency and despair.

This patient responded to the above treatment and had no further irritations after two weeks.

Study of the rays and the chakra centres governed, can be of immense help when faced with difficult cases showing little signs of major chakra imbalance and physical abnormalities.

NAME	JEFFERY	ADDRESS	SOUTH AFICA.		FEES
D.O.B	LATE 20's	SYMPTOMS	SEVERE GENERAL SKIN IRRITATION WITH NO VISIBLE SYMPTOMS. ONSET 1 YR. AGO.	DATE	
				G.T.R.	

DEGREE OF DEVIATION FROM FUNCTIONAL PERFECTION

STRUCTURE — DEGREE AT WORST POINT: 0 10 20 30 40 50 60 70 80 90 100

- AURAL
- VISUAL
- C.N.S.
- SYMP. NER
- PARA. SYMP. NER
- ENDOCRINE
- RESPIRATORY
- CARDIO · VASCULAR
- GASTRO INTESTINAL
- LIVER
- URINARY
- ADRENAL
- GENITAL
- BLOOD
- LYMPH
- SKELETAL
- MUSCULAR
- TISSUES
- CELLS
- SKIN
- FLUIDS
- TEETH
- TONSILS

DEGREE OF DEVIATION FROM THE CAUSAL BODY ENERGIES AFFECTING OPTIMUM FUNCTION OF ___

CAUSAL RAY 7

Scale: UNDERACTIVITY 100 90 80 70 60 50 40 30 20 10 — OPTIMUM — 10 20 30 40 50 60 70 80 90 100 OVERACTIVITY — FACTOR

		FACTOR
MENTAL	-+-	OVERSTIM.
ASTRAL	-+-	HYPERSENS.
ETHERIC	-+-	INFLAM.
NADIS		INFLAM.
	PERSONAL RAY 5	
CROWN		UN CO-ORD
AJNA/BROW		OVERSTIM.
THROAT		OVERSTIM.
HEART		CONGESTION
M 4	SOLAR PLEXUS	CONGESTION
A 4	SACRAL	OVERSTIM.
	BASE	CONGESTION
P/E 5	SPLEEN	OVERSTIM.
	ALTA MAJOR	OVERSTIM.

DEGREES OF OTHER FACTORS — 10 20 30 40 50 60 70 80 90 100

MIASMS TYPE	
DET. EFF. OF VACC.	
POISON	
TOXINS	
AUTOINTOXICATION	

NOTES

MENTAL AND ASTRAL RAYS INCOMPATABLE WITH CAUSAL AND PERS. RAYS THUS CAUSING OVERSTIM. AND INFLAMATION IN THE SUBTLE BODIES.

SUGGESTED POSITIVE & NEGATIVE TREATMENTS FOR RAY INFLUENCES

	RAY	CHAKRA	METAL	COLOUR	PLANET	GEM	FLOWER REMEDY	
1	WILL OR POWER	CROWN	GOLD	RED	SUN	RUBY	CHICORY BEECH VERVAIN VINE ROCKWATER	OVERCARE
2	LOVE AND WISDOM	HEART	TIN	BLUE	JUPITER	MOONSTONE	ROCK ROSE ASPEN MIMULUS CHERRY PLUM RED CHESTNUT	FEAR
3	ACTIVE INTELLIGENCE	THROAT	IRON	YELLOW	MARS	CORAL	WATER VIOLET IMPATIENS HEATHER	LONELINESS
4	HARMONY - CONFLICT	BROW	SILVER	ORANGE	MOON	PEARL	WILLOW LARCH CRAB APPLE PINE SWEET CHESTNUT ELM STAR BETHLEHEM OAK	DESPONDENCY DESPAIR
5	LOWER CONCRETE MIND	SACRAL	QUICK SILVER	GREEN	MERCURY	EMERALD	AGRIMONY CENTAURY WALNUT HOLLY	OVERSENSITIVITY
6	DEVOTION	SOLAR PLEXUS	LEAD	VIOLET	SATURN	SAPPHIRE	CHESTNUT BUD OLIVE HONEYSUCKLE MUSTARD WILD ROSE CLEMATIS WHITE CHESTNUT	LACK OF INTEREST
7	MAGIC AND ORDER	BASE	COPPER	INDIGO	VENUS	DIAMOND	CERATO WILD OAT GENTIAN GORSE HORNBEAM SCLERANTHUS	UNCERTAINTY

An example is the case of 'Jeffery', the subtle anatomy sheet is shown and some brief notes on causes and treatments show how the incompatibility of rays in this case was the basic causative factor of the illness.

The chart on page 114 giving suggested treatment for rays also shows gems, colours, metals as well as the flower remedies, and should be used as a guide only. Experience has shown that the gem stones and their cosmic vibration are particularly useful for progressing a person on their rays of life, as is the use of metals and elements.

For the gem theory of medicine, I recommend readers to: *Gem Therapy* by A.K. Bhattacharya.

Progression for our patients is of prime importance, and our thinking must now be directed at progressive treatments rather than purely remedial at a physical level.

I have found that detrimental attitudes, emotions and reactiveness when treated radionically cannot be totally eliminated. What actually happens is that the projected potencies expand tolerance of situations, and the patient's ills slowly dissipate.

The old school of thinking of radionically eliminating a miasm or restoring a chakra centre is not enough. Practitioners must study the subtle anatomy and rays and establish why initially the chakra centre is congested or blocked. The elementary restoration method will not cure in the long term. Progression of awareness is necessary by projecting to patients in order to expand their consciousness and return them to their true paths of life and necessary experiences.

Detrimental experiences that have to be tolerated by patients as a soul dictate can be helped by expanding tolerance with the use of the correct progressive Dr Bach Flower Remedy or the gem stone.

Gem stones contain cosmic vibration of colours, and can be administered in homoeopathic form by simulation techniques on the M.G.A. instruments. Simulator cards are available for gem stones and planetary influences, and the therapeutic value of this treatment when given to the patient in varying potency ranges, stimulates the response to the guiding forces and energies from the solar system, of which we are all part.

THE CENTRAL IDENTITY OF AN INDIVIDUAL
SHOWING THE CAUSAL BODY RAY INFLUENCED BY
THE RAY ASPECTS AND ATTRIBUTES OF THE PAST

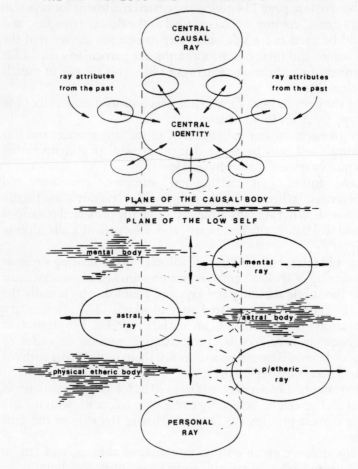

THE CAUSAL BODY ENERGIES ENDEAVOR TO BRING
MENTAL ASTRAL AND P/E BODIES INTO LINE, AND DEVELOP
A PERSONAL RAY COMPATABLE WITH CAUSAL BODY DICTATES

The simulator card with its centre point of focus and the proportional radii is like the sun as the centre of the universe with its series of attendant planets held in magnetic rapport in their orbits giving governed proportions of energy to us all.

A governed proportion or potency of a gem stone or planetary influence will, when administered to the patient, remove the restrictive barriers and restore the natural boundaries of energy, the magnetism being the carrier wave.

The planets, Uranus, Neptune and Pluto are not included in the septenary systems handed down to us from the ancients, but there is some evidence for linking Uranus with the sun in rulership of metals and jewels, and Neptune with the moon. These outermost planets do appear to affect the subtle bodies, and people strongly affected by their influence should respond readily to gem therapy and colour healing.

It is also possible that the influence of planets manifests through some of the powerful allopathic drugs which have a profound effect on the emotional and mental states of patients.

Here, perhaps, is a subtle clue to the working of the hierachy and the universal order of things to come, although there is concern by many of the widespread use of these drugs today. It may well be that through the very fact humanity is being led to a deeper understanding of the close interrelation of the soul and body. It is interesting that an emergence of deep thinking people among the general populace has occured during the last twenty five years. Pluto, traditionally, the planet of the underworld and ruler of all that which is hidden in the subconscious and super conscious, was passing through Virgo, the sign of health and medicine between 1956 and 1972. Uranus, often known as the 'lightening flash', the planet of spiritual awakening, was also passing through this sign, which is closely linked with the etheric world.

This is probably a contributory factor explaining why so many individuals have been shaken out of spiritual lethargy and are now seeking their true spiritual origins.

COLOUR AND ITS THERAPEUTIC VALUES

Life on earth depends upon light from the sun, which is the ultimate source of all energy on the planet. Plant growth, animal development, behaviour and man's own physical and bio-chemical systems depend directly or indirectly upon light energy.

The cycles of night and day and the changing light patterns of the seasons have a profound effect upon all life around us.

This bond between man and the sun is an all-powerful, all encompassing one, linking each of us to the scheme of the universe, and subjecting us to the same natural laws as the tiniest microscopic organisms and cells, as well as the giant stars and planets of this universe.

What is not so readily recognisable is that the colours of which 'white' sunlight is composed, each have their individual effect upon living systems. The physicist Isaac Newton discovered in 1665 that sunlight can be resolved by projection through a triangular prism into seven basic colours which follow an invariable sequence. Red, orange, yellow, green, blue, indigo and violet.

These visible colours form only one small segment of the electro-magnetic spectrum, which extends from the shortest cosmic rays up to long radio waves. The wavelength of the spectral colours are measured in angstrom unit (A) which are one tenth of a millimicron.

The colour range from Red at 7600-6300 A, to Violet 4500 – 3800 A are available in simulator cards from Magneto Geometric Applications.

It is interesting to note that just beyond the visible red end of the spectrum are the infra-red rays and extending beyond the violent end are the ultra-violet rays, followed by X rays and so forth. Science and medicine have recognised the powerful effects both of the infra-red and ultra-violet portions of the spectrum that they exert on living organisms. Hospitals are equipped with instruments that produce electromagnetic radiation of longer and shorter wavelengths than visible light, X ray therapy being the most prominent example. Yet the influence of the visible part of the spectrum colours has been ignored by orthodoxy, yet here is therapeutic value in healing, as we use potencies and proportions of these colour wave lengths on the subtle bodies of man.

Colours have particular relationships to ray and chakra centres. The radionic practitioner can determine which colour will stimulate or sedate a chakra and the colours given in the chart related to centres is to be used as a guide only.

The colour related to a ray is to be interpreted as the carrier wave of that ray information, expressing itself through a particular chakra centre. Treating with colour is to select an individual colour for the particular factor causing the disturbance of the subtle body or chakra centre. Potencies of colour cards can be projected or given orally to patients.

Always establish which colour or colours in combination will open up the chakra centre to the awakened state and yet help to stimulate or sedate the endocrine function governed by that centre.

Blues, greens, yellows are cooling, calming and cleansing. They are also anti-inflammatory.

Red, orange and the darker shades are stimulating and invigorating to the subtle bodies and chakras.

Remember also, that potencies of homoeopathic remedies emit colour vibration and as the potency changes so does the colour emitted.

CHAPTER THIRTEEN

Signs, Salts and Polychrest Remedy

"The universe is a vital wholeness, and owing to the laws of correspondences, each individual, each planet, and every mineral can be definitely associated with these things with which they have affinities, and which react to similar vibrations."

E.F.W. Powell (D.Sc.)

The above quotation should be borne in mind by every reader, whether laymen, health care professional, doctor or astrologer. Only when we bring into alignment the various fields of knowledge, however diverse they may seem on the surface, only then shall we move nearer to the truth.

Each human being is a unique individual with his own particular habits, desires, tendencies and antipathies, physical and mental makeup as well as chemical make up. It is this chemistry within the body which acts and responds to all the subtle anatomy energies in which we should also show interest.

The bio-chemic system of healing with tissue salts originated by Dr W.H. Scheussler, has a definite link with the planetary influences on man and the sun sign under which the person is born. The human body has, as part of its construction, combinations of twelve inorganic salts, and is influenced by combinations of planets and the twelve signs of the zodiac.

Each organ of the body is composed of millions of cells, their composition, structure and type depending upon the organ of which they form part. As an example, the shape and chemical composition of a heart cell is different from the shape and chemical composition of a lung cell. Each cell however small is really one separate and individual life, capable of selecting from the chemically laden bloodstream the mineral that it requires for its development and growth.

This seems to indicate that cells possess some form of intelligence, and respond to thought forms. If a cell requires calcium for its maintenance and growth it will select this from the bloodstream and ignore the iron. It follows then, that if the blood is supplied with the foods which contain the elements for growth and repair, each cell will extract the required mineral for its own survival.

A carefully balanced diet containing the various elements required by the body is essential to well-being.

All these elements are to be found in natural foods, vegetables, fruits, cereals, herbs, roots, eggs, etc.

Vegetables and fruits being rich in the vital cell salts, are of vast importance to man as these salts supply the cells with the material required for their existence.

Without these mineral substances in the bloodstream the body would not survive. Paracelus of old said 'The blood is life', and quality of the blood stream is to some extent controlled by the food we eat and our bio-chemic make-up.

Turning to the astrological link, we find that the sun rules the vital fluids in the body, it is also the source of life and vital powers. In order to keep the blood in perfect condition it is necessary to ensure an adequate supply of the particular chemical salt which is indicated by the position of the sun at the time of birth.

We know that there are twelve signs of the zodiac and twelve houses of the horoscope.

The human body can also be divided into twelve parts, or 30° for each part within the 360° of the whole, each part having an affinity with one of the divisions of the zodiac or the houses of the horoscope.

We have twelve bio-chemic salts and each has an affinity with a particular sign of the zodiac and one of the divisions within the human body.

In order to determine which of the salts are most likely to be deficient in any particular patient it is necessary to determine the

ZODIAC SIGN	PLANET RULER	RAY NO.	CELL SALT	HOM. REMEDY
Aries	Mars	3	Kali Phos	Aconite
Taurus	Venus	7	Nat. Sulph.	Belladonna
Gemini	Mercury	5	Kali Mur	Bryonia
Cancer	Moon	4	Calc. Fluor	Ipececuanha
Leo	Sun	1	Mag. Phos	Chamomilla
Virgo	Mercury	5	Kali Sulph	Pulsatilla
Libra	Venus	7	Nat. Phos	Rhus Tox.
Scorpio	Mars/Pluto	3	Calc. Sulph	Pulsatilla
Sagittarius	Jupiter	2	Silica	Mercurius
Capricorn	Saturn	6	Calc Phos	Sulphur
Aquarius	Saturn/Uranus	6	Nat. Mur	Arsenicum Alb.
Pisces	Jupiter/Neptune	2	Ferrum Phos.	Veratrum Alb.

sign in which the sun is placed at the time of birth and if affected by any of the planets and, if so, the place of those planets in the horoscope. By careful balancing, or dowsing and reference to the chart this information can be obtained.

Every bio-chemic tissue salt has not only a relationship with the zodiac sign, but also with a homoeopathic remedy or polychrest.

The polychrest or general remedy which is useful in many conditions will greatly enhance the practitioner's ability, as the homoeopathic remedies linked with the zodiac signs and salts give a sound base for prescribing with safety.

This chart of the relationship between salts and homoeopathic remedies may be linked with the chart on colours or chakras etc.

Here the practitioner has a guide to remedies of therapeutic value, selected from a wide range, but all related to a ray or wave form that is linked within the universe.

Alice Bailey recommends the use of drugs made of herbs or minerals belonging to the same ray of the patient under treatment.

I am convinced, after using homeopathy for many years, that remedies indicated in a materia medica as compatible, or following another remedy well, are actually on the same ray and will work on related energy centres and rays as indicated in the chart on page 122.

Once the patient's date of birth and planet ruler have been established, check if the ray number is apparent in their causal ray or personality. I have found a strong correlation here. Only use it as a guide and not as your norm for establishing ray influences. The full radionic analysis will give you the detail, use the chart as a guide for possible remedy selection.

CHAPTER FOURTEEN

Awareness is Healing

"As man becomes aware of his own Divinity he, from that point on, becomes his own creator."
Murdo MacDonald-Bayne, M.C., Phd, D.D.

Those readers who have stayed with me this far will now be aware of man's spiritual origins, and will realise that disease is in essence the conflict between the causal body and personality. Healing also stems from the awareness, that to know yourself is to recognise the causes, and this applies in our daily practice with the recognition of our patient's causative factors of illness.

Many practitioners of Radionics and Homoeopathy today are trying to equate their therapies to scientific backgrounds and provings. This will only serve to bring about their disproving. These fields of medicine whether labelled alternative or complimentary are born out of universal concepts and not material.

Radionics has to stand with its own foundations and origins, and should not be guided towards catastrophy by this clamour for acceptance by orthodoxy.

In radionics there are those that spend too much time worrying about 'what others think of us' and want to be accepted by this profession or that. Radionics and Homoeopathy would do better in proving to the outside world that a viable system of healing exists, based on proven universal principles which can be understood by all.

Heaven knows we have seen the weakness of conventional medicine, and they are many. Do we as health care professionals working to universal laws want to be aligned with these weaknesses?

All alternative or fringe therapies would do well to communicate and unite under the umbrella of the universal law of healing, but certainly not in the creation of a bastion to challenge the orthodox systems in confrontation in their demand for acceptance.

The joy in life is being aware. The awareness that amongst chaos and power struggles between nations, the inflated egos of groups and some individuals, there is always the universal laws of nature, directing the seasonal changes, commanding the dynamic balance of the myriad of stars in heaven, and reminding man of his spiritual origins.

Awareness of the superior intelligence allows the practitioner in radionics to tap the divine consciousness for the benefit of healing. I said earlier that dowsing and using the intuition when questioning the universal source about your patient will reveal the correct answers, as the universal source was aware of the answer long before the question was posed.

Awareness and the study of spiritual science reveals a truth that is not readily conceived by modern thought, and yet is of profound significance both to the understanding of life and human behaviour patterns.

We are in an age of increasing moral relativity, and the morals of individuals are often questioned by physical laws manifest from the material world or orthodox beliefs.

These moral laws and consequences on each individual reach from one life to another and are implicit in the events of human history. These laws are directly related to man's earthly consciousness and are governed by current opinion and beliefs. What is of importance to the individual is the direct perception apparent in his own life, the inevitable experiences which can have a true meaning and reason for his very existence. He is aware of his inner self and his individuality, and yet the feeling of belonging to the realm of spirit makes loneliness impossible. If mens minds were more aware of the conviction that there is a natural and moral order existing in the universe, controlled by a superior intelligence, which, if disregarded only continues their unending frustration, suffering and conflict, there would, I believe, take place a revolution in western civilisation more fundamental than that of communism and national socialism. We have already seen this growing awareness.

Individuals have been prodded from their spiritual lethargy by profound experiences that motivated the change in thinking. It occurs to many when disease and illness wreak havoc on their physical bodies, an awareness of the spiritual and universal laws heals their physical body and uplifts their consciousness. The role of the health care professional is in education of his patient as well as healing physical symptoms.

Healing can be obtained by making the patient aware of his self induced anxieties, traumas, and the creation of barriers to the natural flow of energies. His relationship to fellow man and the other kingdoms of nature, as well as the energies contained in potencies of nature's thought forms. These act as coded instructions to the subtle body, all bring about awareness, harmony and healing.

Already, in our studies on the path to higher knowledge through radionics, we have become cognisant of the higher worlds. Higher levels of consciousness and being. The universal source which interpenetrates our earthly existence and stretches far beyond its boundaries.

IT is to these worlds we pass in death, when we have discarded our physical body and are released to a progressive experience of these spiritual worlds which we cannot evade. But the study during life of the higher knowledge, the acceptance of the superior intelligence, allows progression as we discard the burden of physical and lower consciousness and tap the divine knowledge, it increases our awareness, sharpens the intuition and gives us the truthful answers to our universal problems. We can cross the bridge between the two worlds, by establishing the rainbow bridge between the left and right brain. This study of man and his spiritual origins is enhanced by the use of the radiesthetic faculty and the symbols and rituals, that make Radionics the progressive healing energy.

APPENDIX A

The Peggotty Board

The Peggotty Board is used extensively by therapists knowledgeable in skeletal conditions and the spinal column. The peggotty board is used for all symptoms related to the spine, hips, joints, the locomotor system in general, all muscular and ligamentous conditions.

No dowsing or analytical procedures are involved with the peggotty, it is purely a treament instrument.

Once the condition or modality has been established, a rate is decided upon by consulting the rate book or list supplied with the instrument.

Pegs are placed in the squares in the following sequence.

1.   Work from right to left top row first. The unmarked squares are as follows – Remember right to left 0. 10. 20. 30. 40. 50. Then cross the double lines start again 50. 60. 70. 80. 90. 100. (note 50 appears twice).

2.   Work from right to left second row from top. The unmarked squares are 0. 1. 2. 3. 4. 5. cross the double lines 5. 6. 7. 8. 9. 10. (note 5 appears twice). (This procedure continues down the board.)

3.   Always when 50 or 5 occurs in a rate, put the peg left of centre of the board.

The patient's hair sample is placed on the saddle or cradle at the end of the board on centre. The cradle balances on the fine pointed pin.

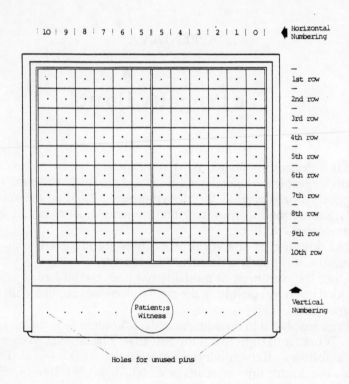

The Peggotty Board.

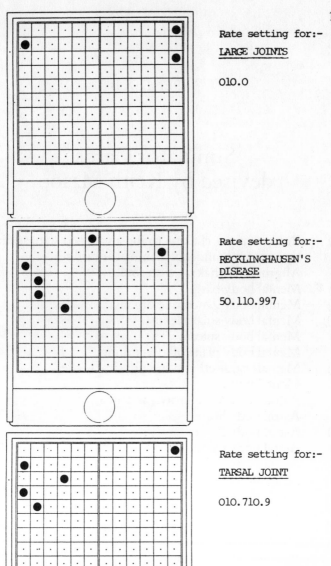

Rate setting for:-
LARGE JOINTS

010.0

Rate setting for:-
RECKLINGHAUSEN'S
DISEASE

50.110.997

Rate setting for:-
TARSAL JOINT

010.710.9

APPENDIX B

Simulator Cards
devised by Keith Mason

(A) Restore major chakras to the awakened state as directed
by own soul influence. Simulator card reads:
Aligment of chakras with soul.
(B) Mental body base.
(C) Mental body generative organs.
(D) Mental body solar plexus.
(E) Mental body spleen.
(F) Mental body plane of lower mind.
(G) Mental/astral/etheric and physical bodies.
(H) Mental unit.
(I) Astral body head (crown and ajna).
(J) Astral body heart.
(K) Astral body throat.
(L) Astral body base.
(M) Astral body generative organs.
(N) Astral body solar plexus.
(O) Astral body spleen.
(P) Astral body permanent atom.
(Q) Physical etheric generative organs.
(R) Physical etheric spleen.
(S) Physical etheric solar plexus.
(T) Physical etheric permanent atom.
(U) Physical etheric head (crown and ajna).
(V) Physical etheric heart.
(W) Physical etheric throat.
(X) Physical etheric base.

APPENDIX C
Teeth Chart

The energetic relations of teeth (or odontons) with respect to organs and tissue systems.

Left side (upper jaw — teeth +1 to +8 / American 9–16 / International 21–28)

Category	Pineal gland	Inter mediate pituitary lobe	Posterior pituitary lobe	Thymus	Thyroid	Para thyroid	Anterior pituitary lobe
ENDOCRINE GLANDS	Pineal gland	Inter mediate pituitary lobe	Posterior pituitary lobe	Thymus	Thyroid	Para thyroid	Anterior pituitary lobe
SENSE ORGANS	Nose	Eye, Posterior portion	Nose	Nose	Tongue	Tongue	Internal ear, Tongue
PARANASAL SINUSES	Sphenoidal sinus, Frontal sinus		Ethmoid cells		Maxillary Sinus	Maxillary Sinus	
JOINTS	Posterior knee; Sacro coccygeal joint; Ankle joint	Hip	Shoulder - ulnar side, Elbow - ulnar side, Hand - ulnar side	Foot, Big toe	Anterior hip, Anterior knee, Medial ankle joint	Jaw	Shoulder - radial side, Elbow - radial side, Hand - radial side; Foot - planter side, Toes; Sacro - iliac joint
SEGMENTS OF THE SPINAL MARROW AND DERMATOMES	SC1 SC2 / SL2 SL3 / SCO / SS3 SS4 SS5 (Posterior)	SC1 SC2 / STh8 / STh9 / STh10 (Lateral)	SC1 SC2 / SC5 SC6 SC7 / STh2 STh3 STh4 / SL4 SL5		SC1 SC2 / STh11 / SL1	SC1 SC2 / STh12 STh11 / SL1	SC1 SC2 / STh5 STh6 STh7 / SS1 SS2
VERTEBRAE	C1 C2 / L2 L3 / CO S5 S4 S3	C1 C2 / Th8 / Th9 / Th10	C1 C2 / C5 C6 C7 / Th2 Th3 Th4 / L4 L5		C1 C2 / Th11 / L1	C1 C2 / Th12 Th11 / L1	C1 C2 / Th5 Th6 Th7 / S1 S2
ORGANS	Urinary bladder left side, Genito urinary area, Rectum, Anal canal; Kidney - left side	Gall bladder, Biliary ducts left side; Liver - left side	Large Intestine left side; Lung - left side		Oesophagos, Stomach left side; Pancreas		Duodenum left side, Jejunum Ileum; Heart left side
TISSUE SYSTEMS							Central Nervous system, Limbic system
OTHER SYSTEMS				Mammary gland left side			
JAW SECTIONS (upper)	I	II	III	III	IV	IV	V
AMERICAN NOMENCLATURE	9 / 10	11	12	13	14	15	16
INTERNATIONAL NOMENCLATURE	21 / 22	23	24	25	26	27	28
TOOTH NUMBER	+1 / +2	+3	+4	+5	+6	+7	+8

Right side (upper jaw — teeth 1+ to 8+ / American 1–8 / International 11–18)

Category	Anterior pituitary lobe	Para thyroid	Thyroid	Thymus	Posterior pituitary lobe	Inter mediate pituitary lobe	Pineal gland
ENDOCRINE GLANDS	Anterior pituitary lobe	Para thyroid	Thyroid	Thymus	Posterior pituitary lobe	Inter mediate pituitary lobe	Pineal gland
SENSE ORGANS	Internal ear, Tongue	Tongue	Tongue	Nose	Nose	Eye, Posterior portion	Nose
PARANASAL SINUSES		Maxillary Sinus	Maxillary Sinus		Ethmoid cells		Sphenoidal sinus, Frontal sinus
JOINTS	Shoulder - radial side, Elbow - radial side, Hand - radial side; Foot - planter side, Toes; Sacro - iliac joint	Jaw	Anterior hip, Anterior knee, Medial ankle joint	Foot, Big toe	Shoulder - ulnar side, Elbow - ulnar side, Hand - ulnar side	Hip	Posterior knee; Sacro coccygeal joint; Ankle joint
SEGMENTS OF THE SPINAL MARROW AND DERMATOMES	SC2 SC1 / STh7 STh6 STh5 / SS2 SS1	SC2 SC1 / STh12 STh11 / SL1	SC2 SC1 / STh11 / SL1		SC2 SC1 / SC7 SC6 SC5 / STh4 STh3 STh2 / SL5 SL4	SC2 SC1 / STh8 / STh9 / STh10 (Lateral)	SC2 SC1 / SL3 SL2 / SCO / SS5 SS4 SS3 (Posterior)
VERTEBRAE	C2 C1 / Th7 Th6 Th5 / S2 S1	C2 C1 / Th12 Th11 / L1	C2 C1 / Th11 / L1		C2 C1 / C7 C6 C5 / Th4 Th3 Th2 / L5 L4	C2 C1 / Th8 / Th9 / Th10	C2 C1 / L3 L2 / CO S5 / S4 S3
ORGANS	Duodenum right side, Terminal Ileum; Heart right side	Oesophagos, Stomach right side; Pancreas			Large Intestine right side; Lung - right side	Gall bladder, Biliary ducts right side; Liver - right side	Urinary bladder right side, Genito urinary area, Rectum, Anal canal; Kidney - right side
TISSUE SYSTEMS	Central Nervous system, Limbic system						
OTHER SYSTEMS				Mammary gland right side			
JAW SECTIONS (upper)	V	IV	IV	III	III	II	I
AMERICAN NOMENCLATURE	8+	7+	6+	5+	4+	3+	2+ / 1+
INTERNATIONAL NOMENCLATURE	18	17	16	15	14	13	12 / 11
TOOTH NUMBER	8+	7+	6+	5+	4+	3+	2+ / 1+

Top table (left quadrants)

TOOTH NUMBER	-1	-2	-3	-4	-5	-6	-7	-8	left
INTERNATIONAL NOMENCLATURE	31	32	33	34	35	36	37	38	
AMERICAN NOMENCLATURE	24	23	22	21	20	19	18	17	
JAW SECTIONS	I		II	III			IV	V	lower
OTHER SYSTEMS				Mammary gland left side				Energy exchange	
TISSUE SYSTEMS					Lymph vessels	Veins	Arteries	Peripheral nerves	
ORGANS	Rectum Anal canal Urinary bladder Genito urinary area		Biliary ducts left side	Oesophago Stomach left side		Large intestine left side	Lung - left side	Heart - left side	
	Kidney - left side		Liver left side						
VERTEBRAE	C1 C2 L2 L3 S3 S4 S5 C0	C1 C2 L2 L3 C0 S5 S4 S5	C1 C2 Th8 Th9 Th10	C1 C2 Th11 Th12 L1	C1 C2 Th11 Th12 L1	C1 C2 C5 C6 C7 Th3 Th4 L4 L5	C1 C2 C5 C6 C7 Th3 Th4 L4 L5	C1 C2 C7 Th1 Th5 Th6 Th7 S1 S2	
SEGMENTS OF THE SPINAL MARROW AND DERMATOMES	SC1 SC2 SL2 SL3 SC0 SS4 SS5	SC2 SC1 SL2 SL3 SC0 SS5 SS4 SS5	SC1 SC2 STh8 STh9 STh10	SC1 SC2 STh11 STh1 SL1	SC1 SC2 STh11 STh1 SL1	SC1 SC2 SC7 SC6 SC5 STh4 STh3 STh2 SL5 SL4	SC1 SC2 SC5 SC6 SC7 STh3 STh4 SL4 SL5	SC1 SC2 SC3 SC1 STh5 STh6 STh7 SS1 SS2	
JOINTS	Posterior knee; Sacro coccygeal joint; Ankle joint Posterior	Posterior knee; Sacro coccygeal joint; Ankle joint Posterior	Hip; Lateral	Anterior hip Anterior knee; Medial ankle joint; Jaw	Anterior hip Anterior knee; Medial ankle joint	Shoulder - Elbow - left side; Hand - medial side Foot Big toe	Shoulder - Elbow - left side; Hand - medial side Foot Big toe	Hand - ulnar side Foot - planter side Toe; Sacro - iliac joint	
PARANASAL SINUSES	Frontal sinus; Sphenoidal sinus	Frontal sinus	Lateral	Maxillary Sinus		Ethmoid cells			
SENSE ORGANS	Nose; Eye Anterior portion	Nose	Eye Anterior portion	Tongue		Nose	Nose	Middle external ear Tongue	
ENDOCRINE GLANDS	Ardenal gland	Ardenal gland	Gonad	Gonad					

Bottom table (right quadrants)

TOOTH NUMBER	8-	7-	6-	5-	4-	3-	2-	1-	right
INTERNATIONAL NOMENCLATURE	48	47	46	45	44	43	42	41	
AMERICAN NOMENCLATURE	32	31	30	29	28	27	26	25	
JAW SECTIONS	V	IV		III		II	I		lower
OTHER SYSTEMS	Energy exchange			Mammary gland right side					
TISSUE SYSTEMS	Peripheral nerves	Arteries	Veins	Lymph vessels					
ORGANS	Heart - right side	Lung - right side	Large intestine right side; Ileo cecal area; Terminal ileum	Oesophago Stomach right side Pylorus; Pancreas		Gall bladder Biliary ducts right side; Liver right side	Rectum Anal canal Urinary bladder Genito urinary area; Kidney - right side	Rectum Anal canal Urinary bladder Genito urinary area; Kidney - right side	
VERTEBRAE	C2 C1 Th7 Th6 Th8 S2 S1	C2 C1 C7 C8 C5 Th4 Th3 L3 L4	C2 C1 C7 C8 C5 Th4 Th3 L3 L4	C2 C1 Th12 Th11 L1	C2 C1 Th12 Th11 L1	C2 C1 Th8 Th9 Th10	C2 C1 L2 L3 C0 S5 S4 S5	C2 C1 L2 L3 S3 S4 S5 C0	
SEGMENTS OF THE SPINAL MARROW AND DERMATOMES	SC2 SC1 STh7 STh6 STh5 SS2 SS1	SC2 SC1 SC5 SC6 SC7 STh2 STh3 STh4 SL4 SL5	SC2 SC1 SC5 SC6 SC7 STh2 STh3 STh4 SL4 SL5	SC2 SC1 STh12 STh11 SL1	SC2 SC1 STh12 STh11 SL1	SC2 SC1 STh8 STh9 STh10	SC2 SC1 SL2 SL3 SC0 SS5 SS4 SS5	SC2 SC1 SL2 SL3 SC0 SS4 SS5	
JOINTS	Shoulder - Elbow - right side; Hand - ulnar side Foot - planter side Toe; Sacro - iliec joint	Hand - radial side Foot Big toe	Hand - radial side Foot Big toe	Anterior hip Anterior knee; Medial ankle joint; Jaw	Anterior hip Anterior knee; Medial ankle joint; Jaw	Hip; Lateral	Posterior knee; Sacro coccygeal joint; Ankle joint Posterior	Posterior knee; Sacro coccygeal joint; Ankle joint Posterior	
PARANASAL SINUSES		Ethmoid cells	Ethmoid cells	Maxillary Sinus	Maxillary Sinus	Frontal sinus; Sphenoidal sinus	Frontal sinus	Frontal sinus	
SENSE ORGANS	Middle external ear Tongue	Nose	Nose	Tongue	Tongue	Eye Anterior portion	Nose	Nose	
ENDOCRINE GLANDS					Gonad	Gonad	Ardenal gland	Ardenal gland	

APPENDIX D

E.R. Settings

POTENCY	DIAL SETTING	POTENCY	DIAL SETTING
1X	40	6C	140
2X	52	7C	159
3X	67	8C	175
4X	82	9C	195
5X	95	10C	208
6X	110	11C	215
7X	122	12C	225
8X	134	15C	250
9X	145	18C	275
10X	156	20C	280
11X	167	24C	297
12X	177	30C	316
13X	178	40C	344
14X	179	50C	365
15X	180	60C	371
16X	183	100C	420
17X	193	200C	468
18X	196	300C	498
19X	201	400C	515
20X	209	500C	529
21X	217	M	573
22X	222	2M	611
23X	229	3M	633
24X	236	4M	648
25X	240	5M	662

26X	242	6M	671
27X	244	7M	680
28X	247	8M	684
29X	248	9M	692
30X	250	10M	699
36X	260	50M	778
48X	300	CM	806
50X	305	DM (500M)	835
60X	320	MM	902
72X	325	2MM	914
100X	362	3MM	926
108X	365	4MM	938
200X	420	5MM	949
1C	15	6MM	959
2C	22	7MM	969
3C	73	8MM	979
4C	79	9MM	989
5C	110	10MM	1000 (000)

APPENDIX E

Rae Extended Range Potency
Simulator – Setting Charts

GRAPH A

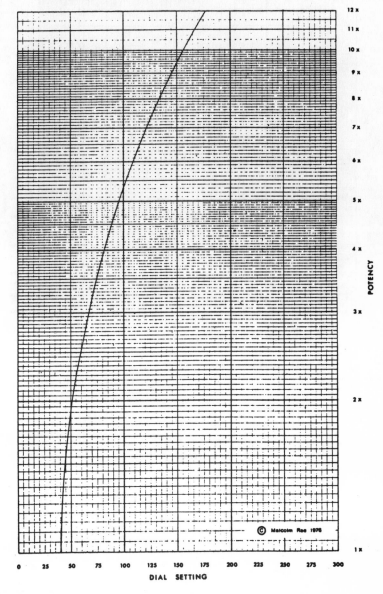

GRAPH B

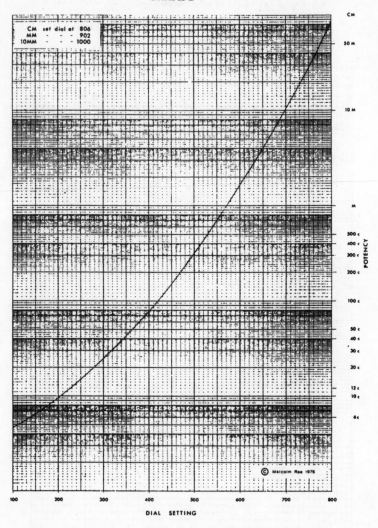

CM set dial at 806
MM — — 902
10MM — — 1000

CM
50 M
10 M
M
500 c
400 c
300 c
200 c
100 c
50 c
40 c
30 c
20 c
12 c
10 c
6 c

POTENCY

© Malcolm Rae 1976

100   200   300   400   500   600   700   800

DIAL SETTING

APPENDIX F

Therapeutic Command Cards

Devised by David Tansley

This set of ten cards is designed for use in the Group Treatment Projector. It was found that the previous Group Treatment Card had what can be described as a moving peak of effectiveness. As more and more therapeutic factors were built into it over the years, it seems that the further the card process grew from its original factors so those aspects became less effective. This of course does not invalidate the effectiveness of the card, but the new set of Therapeutic Command Cards provide a series of specific directives to the patient which are universal in their application, thereby every patient can receive them to their benefit.

Any sequence of Therapeutic Command Cards can be used to suit the practitioner's own needs on a daily basis. A basic sequence would be as follows: T-C Cards 3 – 4 – 2 – 9 – 10 – 8. Each T. C. Card being used immediately after the next to provide each patient with a comprehensive treatment.

T-C 1
To harmonise and restore complete structural and functional integrity to the spinal column and its ligamentous components.

T-C 2
To harmonise and restore complete structural and functional integrity to the seven major spinal chakras and the endocrine glands they govern.

T-C 3

To render all syphilitic, tubercular and cancerous taints (miasms) in the physical, etheric, astral and mental bodies neutral and to eject them from the living organism.

T-C 4

To render all pathogenic viruses and bacteria including their toxins neutral and eject them from the living organism.

T-C 5

To render all unspecified food additives and preservatives neutral and eject them from the living organism.

T-C 6

To render all unspecified noxious chemical and gaseous toxins neutral and eject them from the living organism.

T-C 7

To calm and harmonise the mental, emotional and etheric bodies and induce undisturbed, refreshing, restoring sleep in complete safety.

T-C 8

To remove all congestion from the spleen chakra and the spleen and harmonise the reception, assimilation and distribution of prana by the etheric body.

T-C 9

To remove all congestion, over-stimulation and unco-ordination from the mental, astral, etheric and physical bodies.

T-C 10

To harmonise and restore complete structural and functional integrity to dense and loose connective tissue, connective tissue fibres and to the ground substance of connective tissue.

GROUP TREATMENT INSTRUMENT

When using the control unit with the slide projector and the therapeutic command cards, the procedure is as follows:

Use the control unit button "constant" this causes the instrument to be operational all the time. Use a separate timer for 17 minutes and at the end of each period replace the card in the slot with the next sequence command card. Re-set your timer for 17 minutes and depress the constant button.

Repeat this procedure until all the cards have been in the instrument.

One treatment from each card, in sequence, in sufficient per day.

During the night, weekends or vacation periods, use the timed button only with the T-C card 9 in the slot.

Alternatively use Malcolm Rae's initial group treatment card for out of hours practice time.

One further therapeutic command card of significance is the card called – Alignment of Chakras with Soul, by Keith Mason. (The full interpretation of the card is: Restore all major chakras to the awakened state as directed by the patient's own soul influence).

This command card should be used as an initial treatment on all new patients before the analysis is done.

This will cause the patient to display to the practitioner only the relevant degrees of deviation and thus bring to the forefront of the practitioner's mind the basic causative factors.

APPENDIX G

Esoteric Psychology

Volume One by Alice Bailey

THE FIRST RAY OF WILL OR POWER

Special Virtues:
Strength, courage, steadfastness, truthfulness arising from absolute fearlessness, power of ruling, capacity to grasp great questions in a large minded way, and of handling men and measures.

Vices of Ray:
Pride, ambition, wilfulness, hardness, arrogance, desire to control others, obstinacy, anger.

Virtues to be acquired:
Tenderness, humility, sympathy, tolerance, patience.

This has been spoken of as the ray of power, and is correctly so called, but if it were power alone, without wisdom and love, a destructive and disintegrating force would result. When however the three characteristics are united, it becomes a creative and governing ray. Those on this ray have strong will power, for either good·or evil, for the former when the will is directed by wisdom and made selfless by love. The first ray man will always "come to the front" in his own line. He may be the burglar or the judge who condemns him, but in either case he will be at the head of his profession. He is the born leader in any and every public career, one to trust and lean on, one to defend the weak and put down oppression, fearless of consequences and utterly indifferent to comment. On the other hand, an unmodified first ray can produce a man of unrelenting cruelty and hardness of nature.

The first ray man often has strong feeling and affection, but he does not readily express it; he will love strong contrasts and masses of colour, but will rarely be an artist; he will delight in great orchestral effects and crashing choruses, and if modified by the fourth, sixth or seventh rays, may be a great composer, but not othewise; and there is a type of this ray which is tone-deaf, and another which is colour-blind to the more delicate colours. Such a man will distinguish red and yellow, but will hopelessly confuse blue, green and violet.

The literary work of a first ray man will be strong and trenchant, but he will care little for style or finish in his writings. Perhaps examples of this type would be Luther, Carlyle, and Walt Whitman. It is said that in attempting the cure of disease the best method for the first ray man would be to draw health and strength from the great fount of universal life by his will power, and then pour it through the patient. This, of course, presupposes knowledge on his part of occult methods.

The characteristic method of approaching the great Quest on this ray would be by sheer force of will. Such a man would, as it were, take the kingdom of heaven "by violence". We have seen that the born leader belongs to this ray, wholly or in part. It makes the able commander-in-chief, such as Napoleon or Kitchener. Napoleon was first and fourth rays, and Kitchener was first and seventh, the seventh ray giving him his remarkable power of organisation.

THE SECOND RAY OF LOVE – WISDOM

Special Virtues:
Calm, strength, patience and endurance, love of truth, faithfulness, intuition, clear intelligence, and a serene temper.

Vices:
Over absorption in study, coldness, indifference to others, contempt of mental limitations in others.

Virtues to be acquired:
Love, compassion, unselfishness, energy.

This is called the ray of wisdom from its characteristic desire for pure knowledge and for absolute truth – cold and selfish, if without love, and inactive without power. When both power and love are present, then you have the ray of the Buddhas and of all great teachers of humanity, – those who, having attained wisdom for the sake of others, spend themselves in giving it forth. The student on this ray is ever unsatisfied with his highest attainments; no matter how great his knowledge, his mind is still fixed on the unknown, the beyond, and on the heights as yet unscaled.

The second ray man will have tact and foresight; he will make an excellent ambassador, and a first-rate teacher or head of a college; as a man of affairs, he will have clear intelligence and wisdom in dealing with matters which come before him, and he will have the capacity of impressing true views of things on others and of making them see things as he does. He will make a good business man, if modified by the fourth, fifth and seventh rays. The soldier on this ray would plan wisely and foresee possibilities; he would have an intuition as to the best course to pursue, and he would never lead his men into danger through rashness. He might be deficient in rapidity of action and energy. The artist on this ray would always seek to teach through his art, and his pictures would have a meaning. His literary work would always be instructive.

The method of healing, for the second ray man, would be to learn thoroughly the temperament of the patient as well as to be thoroughly conversant with the nature of the disease, so as to use his will power on the case to the best advantage.

The characteristic method of approaching the Path would be by close and earnest study of the teachings till they become so much a part of the man's consciousness as no longer to be merely intellectual knowledge, but a spiritual rule of living, thus bringing in intuition and true wisdom.

A bad type of the second ray would be bent on acquiring knowledge for himself alone, absolutely indifferent to the human needs of others. The foresight of such a man would degenerate into suspicion, his calmness into coldness and hardness of nature.

THE THIRD RAY – ACTIVE INTELLIGENCE – HIGHER MIND

Special Virtues:
Wide views on all abstract questions, sincerity of purpose, clear intellect, capacity for concentration on philosophic studies, patience, caution, absence of tendency to worry himself or others over trifles.

Vices:
Intellectual pride, coldness, isolation, inaccuracy in details, absent mindedness, obstinacy, selfishness, over much criticism of others.

Virtues to be acquired:
Sympathy, tolerance, devotion, accuracy, energy and common sense.

This is the ray of the abstract thinker, of the philosopher and the metaphysician, of the man who delights in the higher mathematics but who, unless modified by some practical ray, would hardly be troubled to keep his accounts accurately. His imaginative faculty will be highly developed, i.e., he can by the power of his imagination grasp the essence of truth; his idealism will often be strong; he is a dreamer and a theorist, and from his wide views and great caution he sees every side of a question clearly. This sometimes paralyses his action. He will make a good business man; as a soldier he will work out a problem in tactics at his desk, but is seldom great in the field.

As an artist his technique is not fine, but his subjects will be full of thought and interest. He will love music, but unless influenced by the fourth ray he will not produce it. In all walks of life he is full of ideas, but is too impractical to carry them out.

One type of this ray is unconventional to a degree, slovenly, unpunctual and idle, and regardless of appearances. If influenced by the fifth ray as the secondary ray, this character is entirely changed. The third and the fifth rays make the perfectly balanced historian who grasps his subject in a large way and verifies every detail with patient accuracy. Again the third and the fifth rays together make the truly great mathematician who soars into heights of abstract thought and calculation, and who can also bring his results down to practical scientific use. The literary style of the third ray man is too often vague and involved, but if influenced by the first, fourth, fifth or seventh rays, this is changed, and under the fifth he will be a master of the pen.

The curing of disease by the third ray man would be by the use of drugs made of herbs or minerals belonging to the same ray as the patient whom he desires to relieve.

The method of approaching the great Quest, for this ray type, is by deep thinking on philosophic or metaphysical lines till he is led to the realisation of the great Beyond and of the paramount importance of treading the Path that leads thither.

THE FOURTH RAY – HARMONY THROUGH CONFLICT

Special Virtues:
Strong affections, sympathy, physical courage, generosity, devotion, quickness of intellect and perception.

Vices:
Self centredness, worrying, inaccuracy, lack of moral courage, strong passions, indolence, extravagance.

Virtues to be acquired:
Serenity, confidence, self control, purity, unselfishness, accuracy, mental and moral balance.

This has been called the "ray of struggle" for on this ray the qualities of rajas (activity) and tamas (inertia) are so strangely equal in proportion that the nature of the fourth ray man is torn with their combat, and the outcome, when satisfactory, is spoken of as the "Birth of Horus", of the Christ, born from the throes of constant pain and suffering.

Tamas induces love of ease and pleasure, a hatred of causing pain amounting to moral cowardice, indolence, procrastination, a desire to let things be, to rest, and to take no thought of the morrow. Rajas is fiery, impatient, ever urging to action. These contrasting forces in the nature make life one perpetual warfare and unrest for the fourth ray man; the friction and the experience gained thereby may produce very rapid evolution, but the man may as easily become a ne'er-do-well as a hero.

It is the ray of the dashing cavalry leader, reckless of risks to himself or his followers. It is the ray of the man who will lead a forlorn hope, for in moments of excitement the fourth ray man is entirely dominated by rajas; of the wild speculator and gambler, full of enthusiasm and plans, easily overwhelmed by sorrow or failure, but as quickly recovering from all reverses and misfortunes.

It is pre-eminently the ray of colour, of the artist whose colour is always great, though his drawing will often be defective. (Watts was fourth and second rays.) The fourth ray man always loves colour, and can generally produce it. If untrained as an artist, a colour sense is sure to appear in other ways, in choice of dress or decorations.

In music, fourth ray compositions are always full of melody, and the fourth ray man loves a tune. As a writer or poet, his work will often be brilliant and full of picturesque word-painting, but inaccurate, full of exaggerations, and often pessimistic. He will generally talk well and have a sense of humour, but he varies between brilliant conversations and gloomy silences, according to his mood. He is a delightful and difficult person to live with.

In healing, the best fourth ray method is massage and magnetism, used with knowledge.

The method of approaching the Path will be by self-control, thus gaining equilibrium amongst the warring forces of the nature. The lower and extremely dangerous way is by Hatha Yoga.

THE FIFTH RAY – LOWER CONCRETE MIND

Special Virtues:
Strictly accurate statements, justice without mercy, perseverance, common sense, uprightness, independence, keen intellect.

Vices:
Harsh criticism, narrowness, arrogance, unforgiving temper, lack of sympathy and reverence, prejudice.

Virtues to be acquired:
Reverence, devotion, sympathy, love and wide mindedness.

This is the ray of science and of research. The man on this ray will possess keen intellect, great accuracy in detail, and will make unwearied efforts to trace the smallest fact to its source, and to verify every theory. He will generally be extremely truthful, full of lucid explanation of facts, though sometimes pedantic and wearisome from his insistence on trivial and unnecessary verbal minutiae. He will be orderly, punctual, business-like, disliking to receive favours or flattery.

It is the ray of the great chemist, the practical electrician, the first-rate engineer, the great operating surgeon. As a statesman, the fifth ray man would be narrow in his views, but he would be an excellent head of some special technical department, though a disagreeable person under whom to work. As a soldier, he would turn most readily to artillery and engineering. The artist on this ray is very rare, unless the fourth or seventh be the influencing secondary ray; even then his colouring will be dull, his sculptures lifeless, and his music (if he composes) will be uninteresting, though technically correct in form. His style in writing or speaking will be clearness itself, but it will lack fire and point, and he will often be long-winded, from his desire to say all that can possibly be said on his subject.

In healing, he is the perfect surgeon, and his best cures will be through surgery and electricity.

For the fifth ray, the method of approaching the Path is by scientific research, pushed to ultimate conclusions, and by the acceptance of the inferences which follow these.

THE SIXTH RAY OF DEVOTION

Special Virtues:
Devotion, single mindedness, love tenderness, intuition, loyalty, reverence.

Vices:
Selfish and jealous love, over leaning on others, partiality, self deception, sectarianism, superstition, prejudice, over rapid conclusions, fiery anger.

Virtues to be acquired:
Strength, self sacrifice, purity, truth, tolerance, serenity, balance and common sense.

This is called the ray of devotion. The man who is on this ray is full of religious instincts and and impulses, and of intense personal feeling; nothing is taken equably. Everything, in his eyes, is either perfect or intolerable; his friends are angels, his enemies are very much the reverse; his view, in both cases, is formed not on the intrinsic merits of either class, but on the way the persons appeal to him, or on the sympathy or lack of sympathy which they show to his favourite idols, whether these be concrete or abstract, for he is full of devotion, it may be to a person, or it may be to a cause.

He must always have a "personal God", an incarnation of Deity to adore. The best type of this ray makes the saint, the worst type, the bigot or fanatic, the typical martyr or the typical inquisitor. All religious wars or crusades have originated from sixth ray fanaticism. The man on this ray is often of gentle nature, but he can always flame into fury and fiery wrath. He will lay down his life for the objects of his devotion or reverence, but he will not lift a finger to help those outside of his immediate sympathies. As a soldier, he hates fighting but often when roused in battle fights like one possessed. He is never a great statesman nor a good businessman, but he may be a great preacher or orator.

The sixth ray man will be the poet of the emotions (such as Tennyson) and the writer of religious books, either in poetry or prose. He is devoted to beauty and colour and all things lovely, but his productive skill is not great unless under the influence of one of the practically artistic rays, the fourth or seventh. His music will always be of a melodious order, and he will often be the composer of oratorios and of sacred music.

The method of healing for this ray would be by faith and prayer.

The way of approaching the Path would be by prayer and meditation, aiming at union with God.

THE SEVENTH RAY OF CEREMONIAL MAGIC OR ORDER

Special Virtues:
Strength, perseverance, courage, courtesy, extreme care in details, self reliance.

Vices:
Formalism, bigotry, pride, narrowness, superficial judgements, self opinion over indulged.

Virtues to be acquired:
Realisation of unity, wide mindedness, tolerance, humility, gentleness and love.

This is the ceremonial ray, the ray which makes a man delight in "all things done decently and in order", and according to rule and precedent. It is the ray of the high priest and the court chamberlain, of the soldier who is a born genius in organisation, of the ideal commissary general who will dress and feed the troops in the best possible way. It is the ray of the perfect nurse for the sick, careful in the smallest detail, though sometimes too much inclined to disregard the patients' idiosyncrasies and to try and grind them in the iron mill of routine.

It is the ray of form, of the perfect sculptor, who sees and produces ideal beauty, of the designer of beautiful forms and patterns of any sort; but such a man would not be successful as a painter unless his influencing ray were the fourth. The combination of four with seven would make the very highest type of artist, form and colour being both *in excelsis*. The literary work of the seventh ray man would be remarkable for its ultra-polished style, and such a writer would think far more of the manner than of the matter in his work, but would always be fluent both in writing and speech. The seventh ray man will often be sectarian. He will delight in fixed ceremonials and observances, in great processions and shows, in reviews of troops and warships, in genealogical trees, and in rules of precedence.

The bad type of seventh ray man is superstitious, and such a man will take deep interest in omens, in dreams, in all occult practices, and in spiritualistic phenomena. The good type of the ray is absolutely determined to do the right thing and say the right word at the right moment; hence great social success.

In healing, the seventh ray man would rely on extreme exactness in carrying out orthodox treatment of disease. On him the practices of yoga would have no physical bad results.

He will approach the Path through observance of rules of practice and of ritual, and can easily evoke and control the elemental forces.

CONCLUSION AND COMMENTS REGARDING THE RAY RELATIONSHIPS

From many of the above remarks it may have been inferred that the characteristics of any given ray find closer correspondence with one of the other rays than with the rest. This is a fact. The only one which stands alone and has no close relationship with any of the others is the fourth. This brings to mind the unique position which the number four occupies in the evolutionary process. We have the fourth root race, the fourth planetary chain, the fourth planet in the chain, the fourth planetary manvantara, etc.

Between the third and the fifth rays there is a close relationship. In the search after knowledge, for example, the most laborious and minute study of detail is the path that will be followed, whether in philosophy, the higher mathematics or in the pursuit of practical science.

The correspondence between the second and the sixth rays shows itself in the intuitive grasp of synthesised knowledge, and in the common bond of faithfulness and loyalty.

Masterfulness, steadfastness, and perseverance are the corresponding characteristics of the first and the seventh rays.

APPENDIX H

CHAKRA RAY RELATIONSHIP

DYNAMIC ENERGY RELATIONSHIP OF
RAYS, CHAKRAS AND GLANDS

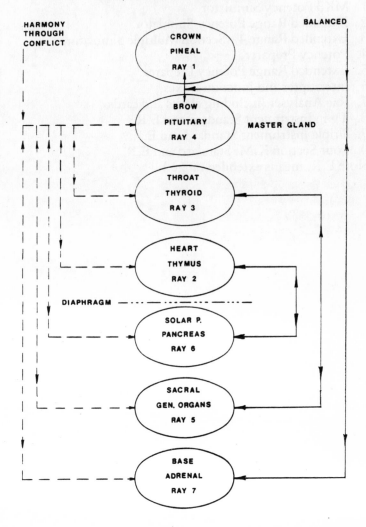

INSTRUMENTATION AVAILABLE USING M.G.A. PRINCIPLES

1. MK3 Potency Simulator.
2. Extended Range Potency Simulator.
3. Extended Range 4 – Section Multiple Simulator.
4. Potency Preparer.
5. Extended Range Potency Preparer.
6. Interrupter and Junction Boxes.
7. Rae Analyser (including charts and cards).
8. Twin Instrument Standard and E.R.
9. Triple Instrument Standard and E.R.
10. Four Section K.M. Standard and E.R.

(Note E.R. means extended range.)

SUGGESTED READING

Report on Radionics, Edward Russell (Neville Spearman Ltd, Sudbury, Suffolk, England)

The Pattern of Health, Dr Aubrey Westlake (Shambala Publications Inc., Boulder, CO., U.S.A.)

The Loom of Creation, Dr Dennis Milner & Smart (Neville Spearman Ltd, Sudbury, Suffolk, England)

Radionics and the Subtle Anatomy of Man, Dr David Tansley (The C.W. Daniel Co. Ltd, Saffron Walden, Essex,England)

Radionics Interface with the Ether Fields, Dr David Tansley (The C.W. Daniel Co. Ltd, Saffron Walden, Essex,England)

Dimensions of Radionics, Dr David Tansley (The C.W. Daniel Co. Ltd, Saffron Walden, Essex,England)

Radionics: Science or Magic? Dr David Tansley (The C.W. Daniel Co. Ltd, Saffron Walden, Essex,England)

Esoteric Psychology (Vol 1 & 2), Alice A. Bailey (Lucis Press, New York, U.S.A.)

For general information on radionics, readers may contact:
> The Secretary
> Radionic Association
> 16a North Bar
> Banbury
> Oxfordshire
> England

For radionic and homoeopathic simulations instruments:
> Magneto Geometric Applications
> 45 Dowan Hill Road
> Catford
> London SE6 1SX
> England

For courses in radionic therapy and seminars on radionics:
> Keith Mason, M.Rad.A.
> Gate Cottage
> Sandy Balls Estate
> Godshill
> Fordingbridge SP6 2JY
> Hants
> England

For information on various alternative therapies:
> The Institute for Complementary Medicine
> 21 Portland Place
> London W1N 3AF
> England

For information on training in Radionics:
> The School of Radionics
> c/o 21 Portland Place
> London W1N 3AF
> England

INDEX

156